W9-CLQ-989

The Artful Journey:

Cultivating and Soliciting the Major Gift

William T. Sturtevant

Bonus Books, Inc., Chicago

01   00   99   98   97   5   4   3   2   1

Library of Congress Cataloging-in-Publication Data

Sturtevant, William T.
    The Artful Journey: Cultivating and Soliciting the Major Gift / William T. Sturtevant.
        p. cm.
    Includes bibliographical references and index.
    ISBN 1-56625-090-0 (alk. paper)
    1. Fund raising — Handbooks, manuals, etc. 2. Charities — Finance — Handbooks, manuals, etc. 3. Nonprofit organizations — Finance — Handbooks, manuals, etc. 4. Endowments — Handbooks, manuals, etc. I. Title.
HV41.2.S78 1997
658.15'224 — dc21   97-19045
                                                                    CIP

Bonus Books, Inc.
160 East Illinois Street
Chicago, Illinois 60611

Printed in the United States of America

Dedication

To my best friend, companion and soulmate, Terri. You taught me how to love and be loved — you gave me the freedom and inspiration to share my thoughts with others. I gladly hold your hand as we cross life's horizons together — you make my journey both meaningful and joyous.

Contents

® Moves Management is a Trademark Registered by the Institute of Charitable Giving.

Chapter 11

Chapter 12

Chapter 13

1

The Philanthropic Carpet Ride

In many ways Morris Moss symbolizes what makes the development business special. He had accomplished much during his business career, and I had come to know him during the philanthropic stage of his life.

Morrie Moss had experienced life's travails and its glories. Through his friendship with Armand Hammer — he served on Hammer's Occidental Petroleum Board — he and his wife acquired a taste for art. He was a Memphis patron of profound proportions. In addition, he was proud to show me the mansion he had donated to a private children's school and regaled me with a story about his visit there to spend time with the kids. He was also extremely generous with Rhodes College and with the university I represent.

Morrie Moss thought a great deal about his charitable giving program. He even wrote about it in his book, *The Importance of Unimportance*. Moss was no master of syntax and the prose will never be described as deathless. But he had something to share. This is what Moss wrote about charitable giving:

> Perhaps the greatest gift of all is not a gift, but a loan. To assist a person in reaching his goal of an education, a career or a business can bring great personal joy and pride to the donor. To be able to help without demeaning the recipient by not giving but lending without expecting a reward, is noble. That nobility can be enhanced by later specifying that the loan is not to be repaid, but instead is to start a cycle of meaningful giving by affording another the chance you have had.

Morrie Moss' giving program at my university was intriguing for what it told me about this rather remarkable human being. While a respectable portion of his giving was outright, the bulk of his incredible support was achieved through charitable gift annuities. What made Moss' gift annuities stand out was the fact that the beneficiaries were all loyal employees of his. Morrie Moss' cook, housekeeper, chauffeur and secretary are now receiving generous incomes because he wanted to repay them for making his life a little richer.

What Morrie Moss symbolized was the fact that the desire to give back can be a powerful motivating force. He recognized that to have an impact means you have to give of yourself. He was a special man, and I am a better person for having known him.

Being better because of an association is not uncommon in the development business. Those of us in fund raising are blessed because we have an opportunity to associate with people like Morrie Moss. We join hands with these special people to further the visions of important institutions and thereby make the world a bit better place in which to live. I have found that reflecting upon this from time to time sustains me through the long hours and the sometimes formidable challenges presented by the fund-raising enterprise. It is a fitting way to start this book.

What I hope to share with you here are concepts and philosophies which have guided my professional activities. I didn't learn these overnight, and, indeed, the learning process never ceases. This knowledge, acquired over many years and through experiences, both positive and negative, are the things I would have appreciated learning more than 25 years ago when I began my fund-raising career. While I benefited greatly from many fund-raising professionals who gave freely of their time and knowledge, our field is just now evolving to the point where we are developing philosophies, theories and literature. It is about time.

But back to Morrie Moss. I start with him because I hope we never fail to see the forest as we navigate through the trees. The trees symbolize practices and techniques such as the ones I am about to share with you. Seeing the forest means we recognize that there is a bigger picture to inspire us as we seek to serve the aims of important charitable organizations. We can never forget the nobility of our purpose and the privilege we have in associating with the Morrie Mosses of the world. If you are in fund raising, this realization will comfort you during those difficult hours and days.

Our organizations are important. They merit the support of the many caring people who are out there. There is no magic formula nor precise script. We will still raise money even though we may occasionally word our case incorrectly. All we have to do is the best we possibly can and the compelling nature of our causes will carry the day. We can always do better, and that is what this book is all about. I take pleasure in joining with you in this exhilarating adventure called fund raising.

2

The Tenets
and Principles of a
Fund-Raising
Philosophy

When conducting a seminar, it is easy to give the impression that you are sharing concepts and knowledge that have guided your entire career in fund raising. The reality is that I spent many years in this business before attempting to wax philosophical. Indeed, I believe that a philanthropic philosophy is ever evolving. You don't start with it. In my case, it came late.

I don't often have the luxury of contemplating the challenges, problems and opportunities facing organizations which seek the philanthropic dollar. Those organizations which are decidedly successful in the development arena almost always demonstrate a certain ethos or standard of behavior. The world isn't perfect. Events don't often unfold in a straight line. Sometimes the good guys lose. But over the long haul I think that successful fund raisers will reflect the following standards:

- *The good ones truly believe in the cause and organization they serve.* There can be little question that you will be far happier in your work if you believe in your cause. It may sound silly, but I also think you will be more effective if this is so. The sincerity and strength of purpose which come from an abiding belief in an organization become apparent to prospective donors.

- *The successful fund raiser always makes paramount the interests of his or her donors.* It is important that this be more than "lip service." Without hesitation the professional fund raiser must recommend against gifts which are not in the best interests of a given donor, and it is vital that institutional and volunteer leaders be supportive in this. The important organizations we serve deserve to be represented in just this fashion. Once again, the ethos of an organization shines through.

- *The effective fund raiser spends less time worrying about competition for the philanthropic dollar and more time considering how to communicate the unique case for support of the organization being served.* Personally, I believe it is in poor taste to sell against other organizations. Why would you want to dissuade someone from making a gift to a worthy organization? I am always happy to assist my donors in making gifts to other charitable organizations, and this, too, has been a gratifying enterprise. If we are good we will always do well enough, and it is certainly true that our organizations will secure support because their cases compel it.

- *The effective major gifts fund raiser exhibits a belief in the economic and political system which makes possible philanthropic activity.* I do not mean that we should cease debating the proper role of government versus the private sector, nor should we become monolithic in party structure. In fact, heated disagreements over philosophy are manifestations of the strength and joy of our system. However, we should never fall into the trap of taking for granted the system that allows our donors the opportunity to accumulate enough to give away and which provides the encouragement to do so. In many criti-

cal respects, fund raising is the ultimate manifesta-
tion of the free enterprise system. As a corollary to
this, it is dangerous to presume that people have an
obligation to give. They don't. To act as if they do
makes us less effective as fund raisers and offensive
to many prospective donors. Wealth accumulation is
a perfectly acceptable choice under our system, and
we should never arrogantly infer otherwise. Even if
you believe in your heart of hearts that certain prospects have an obligation to your organization, it is
certainly not an effective selling premise.

- *The good fund raiser never projects his or her
organization to be something it isn't in order to
secure a gift.* Nor should you ever apologize for the
organization being what it is. Forgetting the ethical
and moral issues, if we pretend about organizational
positions we won't likely win over strong
nonprospects and we may just offend our adherents.
At one of our seminars a fund raiser from an envi-
ronmental organization asked for guidance. She said
that her organization assumed some rather contro-
versial positions and wondered if she should "soft
pedal" those with certain target audiences. Our
response was that she should do just the opposite.
That is, she should accentuate the strong positions
which differentiate her cause and generate the loy-
alty and support. Obviously, extreme views never hold
the biggest audience, but what we are talking about
is differentiating your particular case to identified
market segments. The ultimate example would be
the right to life and freedom of choice groups. Neither
side is likely to win over the slightly less strident
members of the other. I also believe it's important to
have the courage to stand firm on issues of importance to our institutional philosophy. For example,
we must feel comfortable in turning down contro-
versial gifts or those with too high a price tag. We

will surely earn the respect of good people if we remain true to our mission.

- *The successful development professional manages the enterprise as if he or she means business.* I am sometimes concerned that nonprofit managers believe that serving what is thought to be a higher cause requires an approach to management that is deemed to somehow be more genteel. We owe it to all of our constituencies, those we serve and those from whom we secure, to do better than that. I believe it is incumbent upon us to be proactive — assertive within reason. Without the dedication to be the best we can be — the quest to excel — we run the risk of underserving our vital missions. By being too passive, we may fail our donors and our organizations. As a corollary point, we can almost never be too assertive where our donors' or organizations' best interests can be better served by doing something different.

The thoughts just shared with you are admittedly broad in scope. I have also developed some tenets specific to the fund-raising task which guide me and, I believe, enable me to be more effective. I reflect first upon some of Thomas Broce's principles about major gifts fund raising as enumerated in his book, *Fund Raising*. Two of Broce's principles stand out. The first to come to mind is that involvement is the key to leadership and support. The longer I go the more I realize that the involvement of your donor with the organization makes all the difference in the world, especially as you move from a modest to a major gift.

Then Broce stated that cultivation is the key to successful gift solicitation. This, too, is something I believe fervently. Cultivation is an elusive concept for some, which may explain why we often avoid discussing the issue at our professional gatherings. But there is a great deal we can learn and share. Much of this book will be devoted to strategic cultivation and related tactics. These are the keys to major gift fund-raising success.

Broce's list needs to be supplemented. Feel free to attribute these items to my personal biases where you take exception, but seasoned fund raisers will, I believe, agree with most of my points.

- *Giving is top heavy.* This is not likely to change. When I first landed in the development business I was told that 80 percent of the gifts come from 20 percent of the donor base. In reality, it is closer to 90 percent coming from 10 percent. Sometimes the smaller fund-raising effort is a bit more egalitarian, but this principle is consistently verified by major campaign results. In one campaign with which I was associated, the first $100 million came from 110 entities, primarily individuals. Some now say that 90 percent comes from 5 percent, or that 95 percent comes from 10 percent, but my rule of thumb will suffice to make the point. Let us be clear that the 90 percent who comprise the broad base are no less important. I do not judge people by the amount of money they donate or whether they contribute to my institution. And, in fact, the broad base is important because in many instances the 10 percent who give 90 percent "bubble up" from that source. However, for any organization it is vital to identify the 10 percent who will give 90 percent and do those things necessary to nurture their involvement. Otherwise, opportunities are being squandered.
- *Major gifts fund raising is more art than science.* This principle is important because once accepted you become more effective. I know that has been true for me. This was a difficult admission for someone like me with an MBA mentality, but I'm far more effective now that my tolerance for ambiguity is greater. By accepting the fact that major gifts fund raising is largely an art you acknowledge that there

is more than one path to the same successful outcome. Further, you automatically assume a probing
rather than a telling approach. You also learn to seek
input from many sources, discounting liberally, in
developing your strategy, and the outcome is usually
much better. Accepting this verity leads you to a
reliance on your instincts and judgment, and this,
too, will render you more effective as a fund raiser.

- *As a corollary to the above, everyone is a fund-
  raising expert.* It is easy to ignore the professional
  fund raiser. At least that's always been true at the
  organizations I have represented. Everyone believes
  that he or she fully understands how to secure major
  gifts, especially at educational and hospital organizations where egos sometimes take on cosmic proportions. Recognizing that the process is more art
  than science helps because you accept the premise
  that sometimes the nonprofessional will be correct
  in his or her assessment. We should be open to and
  not feel threatened by the observations we receive
  from the nonprofessional. Indeed, input from bright
  and dedicated people can only be positive.

- *Major gifts fund raising efforts are significantly
  enhanced when top institutional and volunteer
  leaders are involved.* Later in the book we will discuss the use of volunteers and staff when it comes
  time to make a gift solicitation, but the point to be
  made now is more general than that. What I hope to
  convey is that the fund raiser is not always the key
  personality and that those who formulate and nurture the institution's vision can often compel involvement. Certainly, these influential people send a strong
  message to our prospective donors. If there is a vision
  of importance to our top leaders, then it often becomes adopted by our prospective donors. We will
  enhance our opportunities for success with the 10
  percent who can give 90 percent if we think care-

fully about the involvement of volunteer and institutional leaders.

- *Donors give to organizations they believe in — whose aspirations they share — not to needy causes.* Let's expunge the term "needs" from our fund-raising vocabulary. People do not give because our organizations need the money. In fact, organizations don't really have needs. The beneficiaries of our services certainly have needs, but even here it is better to sell the outcome in terms of a changed or saved life. This principle helps explain why successful organizations continue to reach greater fund-raising heights. Donors don't wish to be associated with a sinking ship. Rather, they want to support well managed organizations which efficiently accomplish shared visions. Pleading needs is ineffective from a fund-raising standpoint. We can surely find something more compelling to discuss with our prospects.

- *The stewardship function — reporting on the use of gifts and administering irrevocable planned gifts — is too often given short shrift at our organizations.* This is a critical function from an ethical and legal standpoint, but it's even more vital in terms of fund-raising implications. Our best prospects are contented donors, and effective stewardship is a superb cultivational tool. We'll discuss this a bit more when we review marketing principles pertaining to major gifts fund raising, but it is almost impossible to over-emphasize the importance of stewardship.

I hope these principles and verities help you put into perspective the observations, tools and techniques explored in coming chapters. Our journey together takes us from the general to the specific. I have always found it helpful to understand the dynamics which under gird a process with multiple possible outcomes before agreeing to an action plan. It may help you to revisit these important points from time to time as you find yourself surrounded by the inevitable complexities involved in relationship building fund raising.

3

Understanding Your Donors

I am struck by the fact that 90 percent of the philanthropic dollar is directed by the individual, yet until the last several years we have understood little about what really motivates a person to contribute to a philanthropic organization. Some are surprised by the statistic that 90 percent comes from individuals, but a look at the figures verifies this observation.

In 1995, individuals accounted for 80.8 percent of all philanthropic contributions, with another 6.8 percent being directed through estate plans. That's 87.6 percent from the individual decision maker. Few argue with my belief that this is unlikely to change and that the bequest category will continue to grow given the demographics in this country. Of course, corporate and foundation support is significant and of great importance to many organizations. But even where corporate and foundation support is vital, in a mature development program, individuals carry the day. Therefore, it is essential that we understand the motivational "triggers" which prompt philanthropic activity.

The signature work in our field concerning donor motivation is *Mega Gifts* by Jerold Panas. It is a must read for anyone serious about major gifts fund raising. Since *Mega Gifts* was published, subsequent efforts have reinforced the basic Panas findings. *The Seven Faces of Philanthropy* and other such efforts are worth your time. I believe you will begin to see the basic pattern which Panas so eloquently describes.

It is useful to revisit some of Panas' findings as a reminder of what we should emphasize to our donors. Please keep in mind that my list represents a short synopsis and is not a substitute for time with *Mega Gifts*. Let's start with what Panas found to be at the bottom of the list of motivating factors. Sometimes the negative is quite illuminating, and you may find, as I did, that you are spending way too much time with issues of relatively little import. Here is what philanthropists tell us are the *least* compelling factors influencing a positive gift decision.

- *Third from the bottom is the matter of tax considerations.* What I long ago discovered is that tax savings are a means to an end. They allow donors to stretch for a given contribution, or in the case of an ultimate gift, the farthest limits of that which they are capable. Tax and financial benefits can also serve as an attention grabber. But they don't motivate. After all, you don't make money by giving it away. Under the old 70 percent tax bracket (I date myself) it was possible with highly appreciated securities to make money with a charitable contribution, at least on paper. I only found one prospective donor where this applied. When I informed him of this pending bonanza he looked at me rather incredulously. It somehow did not seem right to him to make money with a gift. He later made a very generous contribution, but by that time the tax brackets had fallen and my theoretical windfall was no longer possible. That should have told me something right there. The point to be made is that tax savings are an enabler and not a motivator. I think back to a luncheon with a gentleman whose thoughtfulness led to five separate trusts which are enhancing educational opportunities for future generations of students. He turned to me and said that his initial gift decision was somewhat tax motivated. He had a serious potential estate tax dilemma, and he pointed out that I secured the gift by listening and providing a solution. His next statement was what I remember so vividly. He said that now that he had met some of the students he is helping he would make the gift even if he didn't realize one nickel of tax savings. He claimed that the satisfaction he was receiving had added ten years to his life. It reminds me of Doug Lawson's premise in *Give To Live*. Lawson's book is another great read and is one I have shared with many, including some of my best donors. His premise is that you live longer if you give freely of time and resources. I think that may be true with gift annuity beneficiaries, but for an entirely different reason. At any rate, Lawson cites anecdotal evidence as to the physiological and psychological benefits attendant to giving. I have yet to muster the temerity to solicit one of my donors on the premise that he or she will live longer as a result of the gift. But I believe Lawson has a point well worth remembering. Certainly, tax savings are not the key to giving.

- *Second is the appeal of proposals or promotional materials.* In fact, proposals or slick brochures are really not very important to the process. Do I like carrying proposals when I make a major gift solicitation? Of course. I also like to utilize our promotional brochures. It is just that they are not critical to the outcome and are not particularly motivational. Certainly, they may be reinforcing and provide important educational information. Some studies show that very slick material may actually have a negative impact. I have observed that the proposal is more important to the solicitation team than to the donor as few donors read all of a proposal anyway (with engineering graduates perhaps being the exception). What we have found effective is to highlight in bold face letters the named endowment fund or building opportunity wherever it appears in the proposal. Somehow, our prospects are able to pick out the name recognition. If you are proposing a naming opportunity in a building, the artist's rendering at the end of the proposal should carry the prospects' names as this will likely get some attention. Another technique to consider with proposals is to have a cover letter from the organization's CEO, board chair or campaign chair. While these individuals must be saved for a few upper level solicitations, their presence can be felt with a cover letter. We discovered this quite by accident during a major campaign when we had our proposals accompanied by an introductory letter from the president or campaign chair. The letter would start by expressing gratitude for the prospect's willingness to receive the solicitation team, and then our dignitary revealed his keen interest in the opportunity being presented. A thanks for consideration and an indication of a personal willingness to assist in the process were also included. We discovered that most prospects, no matter how seemingly sophisticated, appreciated a personal letter from such distinguished personages. It is an effective technique. Try it. But you should remind yourself that the proposal itself is not generally of overriding importance to prospective donors.

- *At the bottom of the list is guilt/obligation.* As Jerry Panas likes to point out, people who make major gifts don't feel guilty. They feel wonderful, and this is exactly what they seek from the giving experience. Even some religious organizations with a tradition of pitching guilt are abandoning this appeal. It has not gone unnoticed that the religious organizations receiving mega gifts are those which talk about changing lives and saving lives, not guilt and obligation.

If the three factors just noted are at the bottom of the list of reasons cited for making charitable gifts, what then are the most important factors? Here's what Panas found.

- *Belief in the mission of the institution is the most important factor.* At many of our seminars we invite philanthropists to spend time with our group of fund raisers. The question and answer session is always informative and fascinating. It is often inspiring. Inevitably a fund raiser will query the philanthropist about how he or she selects the organizations to be supported. We hear responses such as: "They do good"; "I believe in what they are doing"; "They are accomplishing important things." Without question, the mission of the institution is of overarching importance to the equation.
- *Community responsibility and civic pride comes in second.* This should really be no surprise. Because of the nature of the constituency involved, this factor is not of great importance for an institution such as the university I represent. However, for many charitable organizations this factor is of understandable significance.
- *Fiscal stability of the institution comes in third.* This is startling to many, but experienced major gifts fund raisers do not find it so shocking. Few donors are interested in supporting the sinking Titanic. I have long held that donors give to well managed organizations (fiscal stability) whose aspirations they share (belief in the mission). The bottom line measurement won't go away no matter how impressive your case statement. If helping the homeless is of interest to you and one of the organizations you are considering drives 40 percent to the bottom line while a competitor puts 85 percent to good use, which one will you support? A major gift is an investment, and donors wish to see it well managed. The old days of the humble but not too efficient nonprofit executive are

over. We must be as professional in the management of our enterprises as are our donors, and everything we do must convey that.

- *The fourth and fifth motivating factors are virtually tied.* Regard for staff leadership and regard for volunteer leadership were deemed highly motivating by the Panas donors. What we tell staff and volunteers is that they are important to the process. Volunteers and staff are the tangible substitutes for the organization. An air of professionalism and a sense of commitment send extremely important messages during both cultivation and solicitation. For instance, a high degree of professionalism helps convey an image of fiscal stability. Isn't it interesting how things start to tie together?

- *The final motivating factor I'll mention is service on a board or committee.* Remember Broce's earlier discussed principle that involvement is the key to leadership and support? Our donors are very clearly reinforcing what Broce told us many years ago.

I have found over the years that in any one major gift situation, and let's recognize that a big gift commitment (however defined) entails a different set of psychological factors than does the more routine contribution, there are several motivating factors at work. I often prefer to deal with broad, psychological categories when determining motivation. It is useful to think in terms of the goals our donors may have for the giving relationship. Prestigious association; recognition; self worth and immortality; memorializing a loved one; feeling good about oneself; and pure philanthropy are a few possibilities that come to mind.

Some of the seminal research pertaining to donor motivation has been done by Gary Tobin and his colleagues on behalf of Jewish philanthropic organizations. What Tobin and his partners have produced is intellectually rigorous and has great value for all of us who are involved in the philanthropic enterprise. I was particularly struck by the profiles of philanthropists as drawn from the report, "American Jewish Philanthropy in the 1990's," published in 1995 by Brandeis University. Some of what the research team found is particularly germane to the tactical tasks of cultivation and solicitation. Here's what the philanthropists told the researchers by both word and deed:

- *The organizations most likely to receive attention are somehow connected to the donor's personal experience.* Of course, this finding is no great revelation. A grateful patient can be strongly motivated, and attending or graduating from an educational institution provides a personal connection. However, we can also secure this sort of connection through creative cultivation. Further, we can sometimes demonstrate to a prospect that our mission coincides nicely with her value system and reflects how she would like to have a lasting impact on this world. The point of all of this is that the stronger and more emotional the connection, the greater the inclination to give at higher levels.
- *A willingness to commit is nurtured and expanded by direct involvement with an organization.* Once again, we're back to Broce's involvement principle. It was interesting that many of the philanthropists indicated that they preferred involvement in a specific project rather than serving on a board or committee. This is good because it means we can be creative in how we involve people. There are only so many slots on "the board" and our donors are telling us that they value involvement in other ways. It will come as no surprise to also learn that the philanthropists were clear in stating that they screen requests for participation as carefully as requests for donations. What this implies is that we must be as careful and as strategic in seeking participation as we are in soliciting a gift.

- *Personal contact with an organization's representatives or constituents is essential for the continued interest and involvement of the major donors interviewed by Tobin and his group.* We are again reminded of the Panas philanthropist who said that regard for staff and volunteer leadership was important. Donors consistently demonstrate to us that interaction with an organization and its representatives is very important. Particularly compelling for the philanthropists was contact with the beneficiaries of an organization's services. An example would be meeting with patients or students. This explains why we urge organizations to think creatively about cultivation. Those hospitals who routinely take donors on tours of various wards have the right idea.

- *The research shows that donors need and want continual and positive feedback about the use of their gifts.* The more personal, the better. Such reinforcing feedback, even a general annual report, was deemed to be a superb cultivational tool.

- *Tobin's philanthropists are very concerned about organizational efficiency.* The ability to achieve a shared goal with efficacy was considered critical. Again, one of our earlier tenants is reinforced. That is, donors give to well managed organizations whose aspirations they share, not to needy causes.

- *Philanthropists tell us that giving something back is a powerful motivational force.* Quite simply, giving, when properly responded to by the charitable organization, makes donors feel good about themselves.

In simple terms, people give to charitable organizations because of a desire to change lives and save lives. The giving process expresses something very profound and important to the donor in terms of his or her value system. It took me a while to realize this because my mentality reflected the MBA approach and I had yet to come across Panas, Tobin and others. I had it wrong for many years, but thanks to experience and the marvelous insights of others I have learned to do better.

I often reflect upon the individuals with whom I have been privileged to meet and their particular set of motivational "triggers." What you unearth can be rather remarkable. I recall vividly visiting with a gentleman in his office on LaSalle Street in the heart of the Chicago financial district. We were talking about establishing a permanent fund to honor his late wife who died of nephritis. Our records weren't very accurate so I was doing a great deal of probing. I asked him about his wife and he offered to read to me the eulogy he wrote for her. I urged him to do so. He began to weep almost uncontrollably as he read the eulogy, and after an appropriate pause I queried as to the exact year of her death. What struck me was the fact that she had died over 30 years before and yet his emotions remained that intense. It did not take a fund-raising course to tell me that he was motivated by the love he had for his late wife and what she brought to his existence. It gave him great satisfaction to know that he could honor her in this fashion. He is now gone, but the fund in her name remains. He did it for his reasons, and the beneficiaries are those who are now being treated for the affliction which prematurely took his beloved wife.

Indeed, the philanthropic journey is fascinating and inspiring.

4

The Major Gift
Dynamic

Let's start this analysis of major gifts fund raising by reaching some consensus concerning the definition of the term. In any gathering of fund raisers representing diverse organizations there is likely to be disagreement about the threshold which delineates the major gift from its smaller cousin. Indeed, units within an organization even define the term differently. How an organization defines a major gift depends upon the scope of its fund raising program, its history and constituency.

What is important to convey is the fact that the process of relationship building fund raising is the same regardless of the dollar magnitude of the gift level which defines what is considered major. But to achieve that understanding we must get past the hurdle of defining what a major gift means to our institution.

Two perspectives should be considered when defining a major gift. The first perspective is internal to the organization. It is clearly the less important viewpoint to consider, but it is real nonetheless. An organization defines the term major gift based upon its fund-raising experience and efficacy. How any organization defines a major gift today will be different than the dollar delineation a few years hence. This has nothing to do with benchmarking the level of inflation. Rather, it has everything to do with "raising the bar" through the ever increasing breadth, depth and effectiveness of a fund-raising program.

The other internal consideration is that of the cost benefit ratio. Major gifts fund raising implies a process which is labor intensive. There are obvious budgetary implications as well. For example, it is not cost beneficial to fly across the country for a $5,000 gift, although we all understand that we might do that if the donor has the potential for a $1 million gift. The point to be made is that only so many hours and dollars can be devoted to the activities necessary to secure major gifts, and each organization defines that level for itself. That being said, there can be no argument that a major gift program, whatever that may mean in terms of giving threshold, is worth it. The payoff is dramatic.

But I've already observed that the internal perspective is the least important. It is now to the more telling viewpoint, our donors, that I focus our attention.

It is critical to determine how our donors define a major gift, and most importantly how they define that term for the organization we represent. Each individual's definition depends upon a number of factors. Net worth and discretionary income are obvious. Also of importance are factors such as an individual's stage in the life cycle, prior philanthropic experience and the giving experience with your organization.

From a fund-raising perspective it is essential to recognize that the process changes when a particular prospect defines a gift as major. I recall a solicitation from a neighbor for a gift of $100 to a local organization. That was a decision I could make myself. I did not need to consult with my wife, nor would she need to consult with me regarding a $100 decision. But had my neighbor sought a $1,000 contribution, I would have demurred. For something that major I would consult with Terri and she would check with me. We would surely consider the orthodontic bills, and we might even call our accountant. It is also possible that I would ask another neighbor about the worthiness of the cause. The logical conclusion is that the dynamic has changed and more factors are at work with the $1,000 decision. The request has reached, as a fund-raising colleague so aptly described it, the "stop and think" level. It will take more to secure this type of gift.

The book *Spin Selling* by Neil Rackham contains some research findings which may shed some light on what takes place when a gift consideration reaches the "stop and think" level. The sage fund raiser recognizes that the process changes and acts accordingly. I have met fund raisers who were incredulous that a long time donor to the annual fund had turned down a major gift opportunity that was clearly within reach. The problem was that the prospect thought of the organization as the recipient of a much smaller gift, whereas the more fortunate organization was placed higher on the priority list. The question is: have you done those things necessary to involve that prospect sufficiently to move your organization up the priority list?

The research described in *Spin Selling* revealed four key factors which are at work when you increase the amount you are asking for. As the size of the gift decision grows in magnitude, you will observe the following:

- *It will take longer for your prospect's needs and motives to develop.* That makes sense. I need to be much more involved and committed if I am going to contribute $1,000 than would be the case with a $100 gift.
- *As you increase the level of the solicitation, the number of inputs influencing the outcome increases.* At the higher magnitudes a spouse, advisor or peer may be consulted. In addition, the decision will need to be carefully weighed against other opportunities and spending priorities. There are just more elements to be accommodated, which heightens the complexity and elongates the process.
- *As the size of the gift decision grows, the discussion becomes increasingly rational, but the decision becomes increasingly emotional.* This fascinating finding illuminated a phenomenon I had observed but could not explain. I recall very vividly a major

donor named Larry. We sought from Larry a sacrificial gift which would serve as the capstone to his involvement with our institution and for which we were sure he would receive great satisfaction. Upon committing to the desired outcome he observed that he could not use the charitable deduction his gift would generate because he had already given so much away. He was right. We developed an elaborate plan whereby Larry would initiate gift payments three years hence, with the commitment being indemnified through his will in case he stepped in front of a big red bus. Larry called three weeks later to tell me he had instructed his broker to transfer all of the shares. When I pointed out his inability to use the deduction he observed that he cared more about accomplishing the shared dream than he did about the financial implications. Not everyone will make the same decision as Larry, but that is not the point. We all factor in both emotional and rational considerations, and where we strike the balance differs based upon our experiences, personalities and stages in life. But what struck me about Larry's decision was the fact that I was doing exceedingly well in addressing the rational, while spending little time considering the dream. It is obvious that someone must love your organization — be passionate about it — to make a sacrificial gift. And yet as the stakes grow it is perceived to be necessary to become increasingly rational in our decision making approach. Don't get me wrong. The rational/economic factors must line up and they can certainly block the major gift decision. **But we must never forget that what will truly drive the positive decision is a passionate belief in the mission of the organization, and we must always address adequately the outcomes to be realized through the particular giving opportunity**. Because of this realization I have changed how I operate as a fund raiser. After lengthy meetings discussing tax considerations and other practical issues surrounding a gift, I am sure to spend time talking about the future generations who will be impacted because the prospective donor cared enough to make a difference. You will see the lights go on in your prospect's eyes, even those who are the most calculating, when you talk in terms of outcomes which appeal to our sense of humanity. I guarantee it.

- *As the magnitude of the gift decision grows the consequences of a poor decision increase.* Hence, the decision maker will take longer to reach closure. It matters little if I purchase a $5 item and it breaks or fails to function. That is an aggravation. But if I buy something for $1,000 and it fails to operate as expected, that is enough to sour the entire day. Major gift decisions take more time simply because the stakes are higher and the prospect cannot afford a mistake. It is important for our prospects to achieve what they expect from a giving relationship with our organization, and they will take longer in reaching a decision to help ensure that their expectations are achieved.

What all of this indicates is that as you cross the threshold from small to major gift, the dynamics change. Therefore, we must do additional or different things if we are to consistently succeed in securing major gift commitments. By defining the types of gift opportunities available to our donors we can more clearly gain an understanding of the strategic implications for acquiring them. Effectiveness demands that we understand these nuances so we can undertake those activities which will ensure the desired outcome. Understanding the determining factors will also allow us to make judgments about where we are with a given prospect and what that implies for the giving relationship.

Buck Smith and Dave Dunlop spent a great deal of time defining the basic types of gifts fund raisers deal with. What was unique about their approach was the fact that they defined these opportunities from a donor's perspective. There are three basic gift types we must consider.

- **Annual or Sustaining Gifts.** I believe the term sustaining is more accurate, but for many of us who have been in the business a long time it is difficult to abandon the reference to annual gift. We all recognize that smaller gifts are often both solicited and donated more frequently than annually. I recall the first fund-raising seminar I attended where a colleague observed that her organization was soliciting its donors more than once a year. Many commented that this would surely generate calls and letters of protest pointing out that there must be something woefully wrong with that organization's record keeping. The development professional responded that two or three such comments were received, but the organization secured another $150,000 of support. At the next coffee break we were all on the phone to our respective offices directing that another mailing be prepared as soon as possible. Regardless of the exact timetable that is utilized, what typifies the annual or sustaining gift is frequency. These are gifts which are frequently asked for and frequently donated. What is truly important is that these gifts entail little decision making from the donor's perspective. These are not "stop and think" gifts.
- **Major or Special Gifts.** These are "stop and think" contributions which are typified by infrequency. That is, they are infrequently asked for and infrequently donated because to seek them on a more frequent basis would not likely be successful. What is truly significant is the fact that this type of gift decision entails extensive decision making. It matters not the exact magnitude of the gift. For descriptive purposes, a major or special gift is often given a threshold of ten times the annual gift. It could be eight or nine as easily as it could be eleven or twelve, but we estab-

lish a threshold so that we pause to consider the process from the donor's viewpoint. If the largest single gift a prospect has made to your organization is $1,000 and you are on your way to solicit $10,000, you need to consider whether you have done those things necessary to involve the prospect so that you have a reasonable probability of success. The decision dynamic is different when you are in the "stop and think" category. Just because someone is friendly and thinks of you as a $1,000 organization does not necessarily mean that you have moved up the priority list sufficient for a gift of ten times that amount. I recall making a presentation to a volunteer group, the chairman of which was somewhat reluctant to attend. He felt that there was really nothing to be learned from my session because he was already meeting with great success. I was concerned that he might be correct because all of his donors were contributing $100,000 or more every single year! As I reached my description of a "stop and think" gift this gentleman interrupted me to observe that the distinction between sustaining and major gifts was worth the "price of admission." He observed that "If what you are telling me is true, every now and then I should ask my $100,000 donors for gifts of $1 million or more." I responded in the affirmative and further inquired, hoping to seize upon a teachable moment, as to whether any of his donors had ever made a very large gift to another organization. He responded that one of his friends had just committed in excess of $1 million to a major university, and at that point it was obvious to me that a light went on in his cerebral cavity. He mused that perhaps every five years or so he should seek from his prospects a once-in-a-lifetime opportunity which is a multiple of ten or more times the annual gift. It matters not whether the relationship is $100 to $1,000; $1,000 to $10,000; or $100,000 to $1 million. What is significant is the fact that from the donor's perspective this gift is in a different category, and you must do some different or additional things to improve your probability for success.

- **The Ultimate Gift.** The ultimate gift results from long term relationship building. It is often a once-in-a-lifetime expression of support, and we like to think in terms of 1,000 to 2,000 times the size of the annual gift. The scenario is often one where someone contributes steadily to an organization and then increases the magnitude of support during and after a campaign. This may happen several times through the years as the donor makes a succession of annual and major gifts. There comes a time when the organization means so much to a given prospect in terms of shared values that he or she does something rather remarkable in furtherance of its mission. Often it entails a combination of outright gift, life income gift and bequest. Perhaps it's a provision directing 25 percent, 50 percent or even 100 percent of a residual estate to the organization. The important point is that an ultimate gift is a by-product of long-term relationship building. Of my list of over 200 prospects, I believe that about 40 (many are married couples) are candidates for an ultimate gift. Their family obligations, net worth and ego identification with our institution are such that an ultimate gift would be perceived as an appropriate legacy. I may not even be there when these gift commitments are finalized, and probably only half of these individuals will finally decide upon an ultimate gift. This is a human enterprise involving numerous influencing factors and much can happen over the years. What is important to recognize is that we cannot necessarily control all of the dynamics, but ultimate gifts naturally occur with major gifts programs.

Dave Dunlop will tell you that annual or sustaining gift fund raising is ask oriented. He calls it "asking or speculative fund raising." This is not meant to be pejorative because this is as it should be. An effective annual fund professional is always asking, whether over the telephone or in the third paragraph of a letter. In contrast, major, special and ultimate gifts are a form of nurturing fund raising. The emphasis is on cultivation and relationship building, while the ask occurs only every now and again. The two basic gift types are along the same continuum, but the techniques for securing them are different.

Annual or sustaining gifts are solicited through the mail or via telemarketing. That is because it is the most cost efficient way to proceed. You can secure small gifts through mass marketing. Some sustaining gifts are secured through personal solicitation, especially where a program is new or the particular constituents are of great importance to the organization. In the case of the university I represent, there is no question we would increase our average gift and our participation rate if we were to personally solicit our over 300,000 living alumni every year. But it is impossible and not very efficient. However, there is no other way to consistently secure the major or special gift other than through personal solicitation. You can't consistently secure "stop and think" gifts through the mail or over the phone. If you know a way, please let me know — I'd love to quit traveling.

Fund raisers love pyramids. Let's compare what exists in a mature development program when you examine both the number of donors and the dollars raised every year.

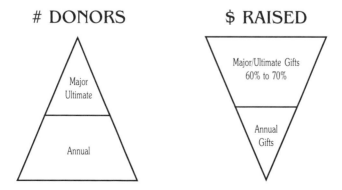

In terms of dollars raised, the pyramid gets turned upside down. From 60 percent to 70 percent of that which is raised come from major and ultimate gifts. What does that imply? If you are to maximize fund-raising opportunities for your organization you must identify the 10 percent who can give 90 percent, and involve them. The 90 percent who give 10 percent are no less wonderful as human beings, and indeed the 10 percent who make those big gifts often "bubble up" from the general ranks. It's just that major and ultimate gifts have such a dramatic impact and you don't wish to "leave the money on the table."

What is significant about these definitions is that they imply certain things about the fund-raising process. Our strategies, tactics and techniques will differ depending upon the type of gift we are seeking. This is more fully described on our progression-of-giving chart.

The strategic implications attendant to the type and magnitude of the gift being sought are vital considerations. Effective major gifts fund raisers are ever mindful of these distinctions and how they affect donors.

	Annual Fund Gift	Major Gift	Ultimate Gift
Purpose	Operational Needs	Buildings, Equipment, and Endowment	Primarily Endowment
Types	Sustaining Gifts	Special and Major Gifts (10 to 25 times Annual Gift)	Generally Once-in-a-lifetime Expressions of Support (1,000 to 2,000 times Annual Gift)
Characteristics	Frequently Given Frequently Asked For Decision is Rational, Cerebral Decision Made Quickly Decision Can Usually be Made Without Professional Assistance Decision Often Made Without Spouse Approval	Infrequently Given Infrequently Asked For Decision Becomes Emotional, Visceral Stop-and-Think Gift Takes Longer for Decision Nurturing Fundraising Spouse Almost Always Involved	May Involve Combination of Giving Methods, Often Deferred Long Term Relationship Building Decision Becomes Increasingly Emotional Takes Longer and More Study for Decision Receives Professional Input from Others The Consequences of a Poor Decision Become Greater
Strategy	Sell Special Packages Special Projects & Activities Seek Broad Based Support and Peer Involvement Begin Lifelong Relationship Acquire, Renew, Upgrade Little Cultivation Required CULTIVATE [ASK]	Market Institution's Mission & Special Opportunities Focus on Select Audience (Financial Capability + Interest + Involvement) Foster Strong Personal Relationship Leverage Association of Staff, Partners, Volunteers Prior and Regular Cultivation CULTIVATE [ASK]	Total Commitment to Institution's Mission Estate Planning Service & Special Opportunities Educate Prospects Regarding Planned Giving Vehicles Create Bonding Relationship Leverage Close Relationships of Staff, Partners, Volunteers Intensive Cultivation CULTIVATE [ASK]
Methods	Direct Mail Telethon Mass Marketing Special Events Local and Community Programs Personal Solicitation of Prospects Affinity Programs	Personal Solicitation (several contacts) Special Events (to focus attention and cultivation) Direct Mail (for information, cultivation) Initiation of Stewardship	On-Going Stewardship Personal Solicitation (a number of contacts) Educational Seminars Direct Mail and Topical Newsletters (for information, cultivation) Special Projects and Events for involvement and cultivation
Recognitions	Giving Clubs Plaques, etc.	Naming Opportunities Lifetime Giving Recognitions Wall "Hall of Fame"	Heritage-type Club Naming Opportunities Lifetime Giving Recognitions

The Progression of Giving Copyright © Institute for Charitable Giving. 1995

3/28/96
kar

5

Marketing Concepts and the Major Gifts Puzzle

The discipline of marketing has a great deal to share with major gifts fund raisers. Phillip Kotler, a renowned marketing scholar, has contributed much to an understanding of this process on the part of charitable organizations. In part, Kotler defines marketing as

> . . . the analysis, planning, implementation, and control of carefully formulated programs designed to bring about voluntary exchanges of values with target markets for the purpose of achieving organizational objectives.

I would add only that the process should also achieve the objectives of those in the target market, a concept with which I know Kotler agrees.

The discipline of marketing helps us understand how our institutions are viewed by our constituencies and how to best differentiate and position our services. The marketing discipline also enforces a donor orientation because everything starts with our markets, as represented by our various constituencies, and what is desired from the voluntary exchange relationship.

Fundamental to understanding the major gifts process is the acknowledgment that giving is an exchange relationship.

By this I do not mean the unacceptable quid pro quo such as the expectation of an honorary degree from a university or guaranteed lifetime care from a hospital. These demands happen rarely and we know what our response will be without prompting from marketing scholars. What is really implied by the term exchange relationship is providing people with the experience they expect in return for a gift. I refer to those understandable, natural and laudable human motivations we explored earlier. Whether it be prestigious association, feeling good about oneself, recognition, immortality or memorializing a loved one, our donors have a right to expect something in return for their gift. **Our donors are entitled to the good giving experience, and it is our job to provide it to them**. That is the voluntary exchange relationship marketing scholars describe.

Not too many months ago I attended a reception and was approached by a woman who knew that I was a fund raiser. She wanted to talk about my business, and I always respond to such requests with enthusiasm. She said that the prior year she had made two big gifts to local organizations. I have no idea how she defined "big" but as we know from our prior discussion, it really doesn't matter. They were big to her.

She said the first gift went to a local hospital, and she asked if the gentleman she was pointing to was on the hospital board. I acknowledged that he was, and indicated that he was also on the board of the charitable organization I represented. She said:

> I don't want to bother him with this, but I never did find out how the hospital used my money. I hope it did some good. Oh, I received a letter from some gentleman, although he misspelled my name, but that still didn't tell me how the funds were used.

"What was the other organization you supported?" I queried.

> The church. And you know, that has really been fun. The pastor has been to see me on three occasions, and

he even took me through the church and showed me
the new organ.

I wondered to myself, which of the two organizations was
providing the good giving experience to which she was entitled? I also considered which development representative, the
one from the church or the hospital, would be surprised when
next year's solicitation rolled around. It wasn't difficult to con-
jure an answer. It is our job to provide donors like that caring,
friendly lady with the giving experience they have a right to
expect. The church has been doing just that in this case and
will surely benefit in the process.

As noted, the discipline of marketing helps us identify
the appropriate market segments. In major gifts fund raising
this is of particular importance. We must ensure that we are
spending our time with the 10 percent, the right 10 percent,
who will give 90 percent to our institutions. There are only so
many prospects we can handle and there only so many hours
in a day. We must spend our time with the right individuals.

A tool which can be useful in determining if we are spending time with the best prospects is the Institute for Charitable
Giving's Prospect Evaluation Grid. Here's how it looks:

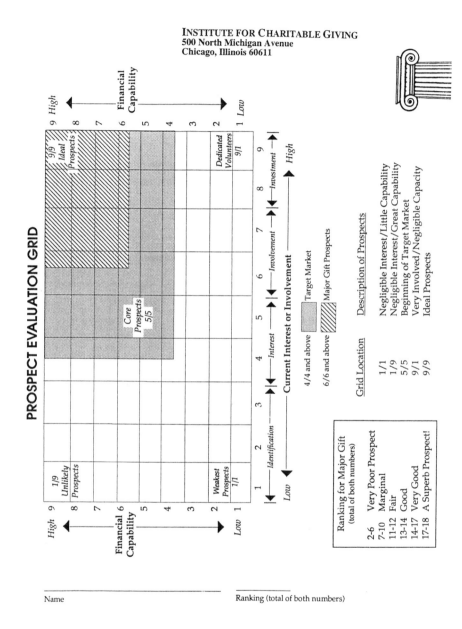

PROSPECT EVALUATION GRID

INSTITUTE FOR CHARITABLE GIVING
500 North Michigan Avenue
Chicago, Illinois 60611

Ranking for Major Gift
(total of both numbers)

2-6	Very Poor Prospect
7-10	Marginal
11-12	Fair
13-14	Good
14-17	Very Good
17-18	A Superb Prospect!

Target Market — 4/4 and above
Major Gift Prospects — 6/6 and above

Grid Location	Description of Prospects
1/1	Negligible Interest/Little Capability
1/9	Negligible Interest/Great Capability
5/5	Beginning of Target Market
9/1	Very Involved/Negligible Capacity
9/9	Ideal Prospects

Name _____ Ranking (total of both numbers) _____

The prospect grid builds on a concept developed by Blake and Mouton, a male and female team of management consultants. The Blake and Mouton managerial grid allows you to plot the styles of managers, all the way from despot to benevolent despot. The prospect evaluation grid applies the idea to fund raising.

The left hand side of the prospect evaluation grid, or the vertical axis, runs from a low of 1 to a high of 9 based on financial capability. The horizontal axis goes from a low of 1 to a high of 9 in cultivatable or current interest. Let's analyze how this tool can be used.

Take a look at the upper left hand corner where a 1/9 prospect might reside. How many times have you walked into a meeting room concerning a fund-raising program, either for your institution or for another, and had someone say something like, "If only we could get Roberta to donate. She could do the whole campaign." Roberta happens to be the wealthiest person in the community. The problem is, Roberta has no interest or involvement with your institution. I remember meetings at my organization where various foundations, such as the Kellogg or McArthur, were offered as prospects simply because they had large sums to convey. The best example was when a prominent family was mentioned relative to the local college of medicine. No one from that family had ever graduated from our institution, nor had anyone been treated in our hospital or by one of our doctors. I then asked if we were without qualification preeminent in an area of abiding and burning interest for the targeted family. In other words, I needed some sort of "hook" in the form of either existing or cultivatable interest if this family was to be realistically approached. That didn't exist, but the name surfaced because of great wealth. Great wealth alone will not suffice.

At the other extreme of the prospect grid is the dedicated volunteer. These warm, wonderful people are vital to many charitable organizations. I could not have survived in my early years in public broadcasting were it not for these remarkable friends who give freely of their time. However, dedicated volunteers can not get us where we need to be for major gifts fund raising.

The annual fund will start somewhere around 5/5 on the grid, and the cross-hatched area is where we will find major gifts prospects, the 10 percent who can give 90 percent. We must be very judicious in the use of our time relative to the labor intensive process of cultivating major prospects, and the grid can help in this regard.

How is the prospect grid used? It is simply a useful tool for any fund raiser to evaluate his or her pool of prospects. A consulting firm uses the prospect grid when it is hired to do a feasibility study. It asks the development professional who provides the list of interviewees to grid each one. What you find is that you begin to self-select. It is not uncommon to put a "Roberta" on the interview list in the hope that a compelling presentation from the consultant can generate interest. It's not a likely scenario.

I am often asked by groups what factors, or heuristics, I use in evaluating my prospects against the grid. As it relates to financial capability, I consider the following:

- *Net worth.* Of course, the higher, the better.
- *Discretionary income.* Obviously, the more the merrier.
- *Number of children.* In general terms, the fewer the better. Children are expensive. For those in a certain category of wealth this is not always a determining factor, but children still receive attention in an estate plan. This is not an absolute, nor are we selling against children. It is just that people are freer to convey net worth when family obligations are minimal.
- *Age.* In a later section of this book I will indicate why I grid prospects higher when they are 55 years and older. It relates to stage in the life cycle and being open to a major release of assets for a charitable organization. Simply, my prospects get more points

on the financial capability scale when they are 55 years and beyond.

- *Prior gifts to any charitable organization garners a higher rating on the financial capability axis.* For years I had it wrong. I used to say, "Darn. Denise just made a huge gift to the hospital. I am too late."

Now, I know better. I say the following:

> Isn't it great that Denise just made that marvelous gift to the hospital. It deserves her support. It will make it easier for me, presuming I give her a bit of time to pay the pledge, when I ask her for a gift twice as big.

The point of this is to convey my finding that giving begets giving. The most difficult gift is the very first one because donors have yet to experience the joy of giving. Also, for those who have made it the hard way or survived a depression, there is a security concern about releasing a percentage of net worth for a charitable gift. Once a gift is made, major donors find that wealth is renewable, indeed it compounds. Getting them over that psychological hurdle can be difficult. Once people give and have a wonderful experience, they want to give again and experience the same thing, perhaps this time with your organization.

Grid qualifiers pertaining to cultivatable interest include the following:

- *Prior gifts to your organization.* If someone has been giving to your organization, regardless of level, give him or her a few more points.
- *Service on board or committee.* If there has been prior involvement, give the prospect a few more grid points. An alumnus, grateful patient, or family mem-

ber of a beneficiary of your services should receive a
higher grid score.

- *A close relationship with a volunteer or staff
  member merits a higher cultivatable interest grid
  position.* Access, especially with top level prospects,
  can be as elusive as the gift itself. Relationships are
  vital, as we will explore in depth later in the book.
- *Spousal involvement with your organization merits a higher grid score if the next step is to seek a
  major gift.* As we will later discuss, big gifts almost
  always involve both spouses.

The grid can help you focus on the right prospects. It is
more a way of thinking than anything else.

Marketing also tells us that gift decision making is
sequential. We go through stages in our thinking to reach a
decision. In *Conceptual Selling* we are told that the elements
of a true donor focus feature the dynamics of a prospect's
viewpoint. Donating is a special case of decision making, and
it occurs in a series of predictable and logical steps. By following the prospect's sequence you find that either there is a fit,
which leads to a gift, or there is no fit, at least temporarily.
The important point is that by ignoring the prospect's decision making process, you will surely lose the gift.

Marketing theorists identify the sequential decision making process under the acronym AIDA. Here's what it stands
for:

- **Attention**
- **Interest**
- **Desire**
- **Action**

Some theorists like to describe it as AIDCA, with the "C"
standing for conviction. It doesn't really matter what you call
it because it's the process of sequential decision making that
is really vital. What this acronym tells us is that you first need
to gain attention in order to be on someone's perceptual map.

We understand how to gain attention. It's automatic where someone has been treated at our hospital or is a graduate of our institution. We also gain attention by advertising, word of mouth and publicity. Once attention is gained, you need to develop interest and then desire before the sought for action, which is a gift to your organization. We aren't conscious of the fact that we think sequentially, and it is not always easy to identify where we or others are in the process. However, I have discovered that if there is a lack of interest and desire, the chance for securing a gift is greatly diminished. The way I have found this concept to be useful is to consider where I think I am in the sequence with a given prospect and plan my moves accordingly.

AIDA parallels very nicely the traditional fund-raising paradigm. When I first got into the business I was told that my job could be generally described in the following manner:

- **Identification**
- **Cultivation**
- **Solicitation**
- **Stewardship**

Notice how neatly the above paradigm fits with AIDA. Interest and desire really equate to what fund raisers call cultivation. This was a subject long ignored in our literature and our seminars because it is difficult to render it tangible or to "get your arms around." But it is vital. In major gifts fund raising, which is relationship oriented, cultivational calls far outnumber solicitation visits, yet we have always emphasized the latter at our seminars because the former is difficult to manage. The techniques later discussed will allow you to manage the cultivation process much more effectively. It is essential that you do so because it is crucial to the outcome.

You should visualize an arrow drawn from stewardship to cultivation. I have discovered that the process is very circular. What I mean by that is that the best cultivation is the good giving experience. Providing a donor with what he or she expects from the giving relationship is marvelous cultivation for the next commitment.

For years, I had this circular concept all wrong. I used to approach our director of annual giving and ask that certain key prospects be pulled from the mailing and telemarketing lists. My reasoning was simple. Within about three years I would secure, on average, six figure commitments from each of my prospects. If, during the interim, each donated approximately $5,000 you could discount the results any way you wanted to and still conclude that the major gift far overshadowed the annual contributions. I did not want my special prospects being bothered by letters or telephone calls during the cultivation process. Well, I was wrong. First, sustaining and major gifts do not conflict. If done properly, they are complementary. Of course, you want to look professional so it is wise to avoid soliciting a major gift the day after the prospect receives a telemarketing call. But the two truly do not conflict. That explains why in many campaigns you couple the sustaining solicitation with the major gift proposal. The other alternative is to space the solicitations. But they do not conflict.

Second, if done properly the sustaining gift actually enhances your opportunity for the major contribution. If you provide someone with a good giving experience it helps involve him or her in a positive way. Obviously, a good experience with a sustaining gift is not sufficient to ensure a positive outcome with your mega solicitation, but it helps. It is one more pretext and context for positive connection with your institution. Recognition of that phenomenon is inherent in Jerry Panas' suggestion that you thank a donor seven times. Please don't tell Jerry I said this, but you really could thank them six or eight times. The point is to thank them enthusiastically and often. This also illustrates why it is important to be prompt in your receipting. Some organizations try for a 24 hour turn around in acknowledgments, and this makes eminent sense once you understand the dynamics from the donor's view point.

This circularity was recognized by Buck Smith when he first began developing the concept of Moves Management. Smith tried to consider the decision making process from the donor's view point, and the result is what is commonly called "the five I's" of giving:

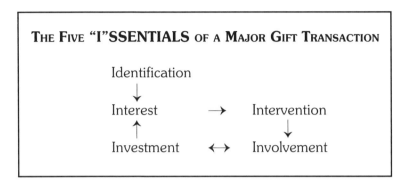

There's a wonderful book, authored by marketing guru Theodore Levitt, called *The Marketing Imagination*. Levitt talks about the marketing of intangibles, and his observations are germane to the world of fund raising. Levitt avers that the inherent danger in the marketing of intangibles is that you will not realize that your donor has failed to receive the expected benefits until it is too late. With a tangible product you receive immediate feedback. Either the microwave works or it doesn't. With an intangible, you might discover too late that the sought for bundle of benefits has not been delivered. The only answer is to stay with your donor to ensure that expectations are met. Once again, the circularity of the process is illustrated.

There is a concept in marketing called cognitive dissonance. I hate terms like that because they unnecessarily complicate the process of understanding. Think of cognitive dissonance as post-purchase or post-gift anxiety. We all experience it, and the higher the level of the gift the more it is a factor. Consider the purchase situation. We know that the people who watch advertisements most intently are those who just purchased the product. It is natural to seek reinforcement and affirmation. I remember an incident following the purchase of a television set. Over a cup of coffee my wife pointed out that a local store was selling the TV we had just purchased for $50 less. That is when the butterflies started and the stomach acid started to drip. That's cognitive dissonance. However, human beings have the wonderful capacity to rationalize just as I did when I said, "Yeah, but it doesn't display the channel in the lower corner of the screen."

As it relates to fund raising, the concept of cognitive dissonance is important. What we normally say as fund raisers is something like, "Thank you for your wonderful gift. I'll see you next year." What we really should be saying is, "Thank you for your superb gift. I would like for you to join me in a tour of our facility in a couple of weeks so you can view first-hand the benefits provided by marvelous contributions such as yours." The point is, we must stay with our donors and ensure that they receive the giving experience to which they are entitled.

An understanding of cognitive dissonance is especially useful for planned gifts fund raisers. People are entrusting us with a significant percentage of their net worth, and in many cases, they further trust that we will provide them with security of a life income. And yet, they may not hear from us for three weeks as we process the gift. I have changed how I operate because of my understanding of this dynamic. I might call from the airport to thank them again for the gift the day before and to indicate that I called the office to ensure that their life income arrangement was recorded immediately. I tell them that the accrual on their first check has already started. I might also call a few days after returning to the office to convey the message that a receipt for a complicated gift takes some time, but everything is operative and their first payment will be mailed on time. If a receipt is delayed, call the donor to thank them again and tell them it is on the way. It is natural for our donors to have a period of uncertainty, especially for stretch commitments, and we can ensure a good experience by staying with them immediately following the conveyance.

Levitt also points out the importance of stressing benefits in any presentation. Of course, we will inevitably discuss features in any given proposal, whether in the form of enrollment statistics or square footage in a building. It is just that it is critical to close the loop by pointing out how features translate into benefits in human terms. Outcomes are what are important. I'll never forget one of my generous donors, who was then considering my proposal for a building gift, interrupting me with the following:

> Bill, I've built plenty of buildings during my career. You don't need to tell me about the number of windows and rooms. What I want you to tell me about are the people who will pass through the halls of the building and what they will accomplish. I am far more interested in what goes on inside a building than I am with the structural details.

How could you forget something like that? What an eloquent way to observe that it is important to emphasize benefits and not features.

Levitt drives home his point about selling benefits very compellingly. He asks, "Does Kodak sell the superior luminescence of its paper?" I rather think that remembrance and nostalgia may be more important motivations. It is not the ceremony, rather it is the saved soul. It is not the linear accelerator, it is survival and quality of life. When you market giving opportunities in terms of human outcomes your prospects will stretch to the farthest reaches of that which they are capable.

6

Moves Management —
The Fail-Safe Tool of
Nurturing Fund Raising

The seminal conceptual accomplishment in the field of major gifts fund raising is that of Moves Management. It was conceived by G. T. "Buck" Smith when he was at Cornell. Smith is rightfully considered to be one of the finest major gift fund raisers in the nation and he was featured as such in *Born to Raise* by Jerold Panas. Smith became President of Chapman College after providing distinguished service to Cornell and Wooster College. It was at Cornell that he formulated the idea of Moves Management.

Smith's close friend and valued colleague at Cornell, David Dunlop, has done much to further and refine Buck Smith's initial conceptualizations. For a number of reasons, Dunlop has chosen to amend slightly some of the original terminology lest the concept be considered too manipulative, but I prefer to stay with the original typologies. Regardless of terminology, the conceptual base is the same. Many of us convey the Moves Management concept through presentations and training, and of importance is the fact that it has made a huge difference to numerous fund raisers and organizations. Indeed, Moves Management has made a significant impact on my career. I know of no concept that is as important or empowering to the major gifts fund raiser, and not a month goes by that I do not receive a letter from someone telling me about recent successes due to the implementation of Moves Management. We all owe a debt of gratitude to Smith and Dunlop, and let us be clear that my presentation of the information is a reflection their brilliance and vision.

The Moves Management concept acknowledges the fact that major gifts fund raising is highly personalized. It focuses on the 10 percent who can give 90 percent, and involvement is the key. This explains why Dunlop terms the process, nurturing fund raising. There is no other way to secure major gifts than through personal involvement, cultivation and solicitation. If we could secure major gifts through the mail or over the telephone, we would surely do so. I certainly would because it would make my life considerably easier. Dragging bags through airports is not my favorite pastime. The problem is that I know of no way to consistently secure major gifts without physically and psychologically getting in front of prospects.

Thinking about the necessity for personalizing the process reminds me of an incident at one of our seminars. A colleague explained to the group that she represented a social service agency and that she had read somewhere that a renowned philanthropist was interested in the kind of work her agency performs. As a result, she submitted a $50,000 proposal to this individual. I responded that seeking big gifts from individuals through the mail is not exactly high probability fund raising and that I would surmise her exercise failed to bear fruit. She then interrupted to tell me that her agency received the gift. After the laughter died down, I responded that major gifts fund raising is more of an art than a science and that $50,000 may not be a "stop and think" gift for that individual. However, unless she had a method for consistently securing significant gifts through the mail, in which case I would attend her seminar and change my approach, we should continue to consider the process as one of highly personal involvement.

The Moves Management concept acknowledges that we must take our prospects one at a time. We are talking now about the 10 percent who can give 90 percent, and the effort is surely worth it. Just look at the cost/benefit ratio for mature major and planned gifts programs and it becomes obvious why such individual attention is worth it. There is no way to generically differentiate major gifts prospects. Broad demographics and psychographics work nicely in mass marketing where general attributes are sufficient to trigger a response. It is not vital to be highly personalized for a $50 contribution, but you had better be completely focused on a particular donor with a $1 million appeal. Think about your own best donors, board members or volunteers. They are all at different stages in their relationship with your organization. They all have different giving capabilities, areas of interest and peers to whom they respond. You must take each member of your highest level prospects one-at-a-time and develop strategies which are appropriate to the individual. This is the starting point for the implementation of Moves Management.

The Moves Management concept tells us to take each of our best prospects and consider first the others we need to involve in the relationship building process. For each prospect we need to identify the following individuals:

- **Natural Partners** — These are people who have a natural relationship with a given prospect and who can tell you what kind of contacts would be best. In other words, natural partners assist in building the needed relationships and help you develop your strategy. Whenever we are confronted with a new prospect with ostensibly significant potential, we ask, "Who knows this person?" We are looking for natural partners. With a given prospect you should think in terms of current donors, board members, friends and volunteers who might know her or him. You can also consider staff members, such as doctors, professors and curators. Why are natural partners important? There are three basic things we ask our natural partners to do. The first is to provide information so that we can develop a strategy. If a given natural partner does nothing more than this, the service rendered is valuable. We need a strategy to approach our highest level prospects. We must have a plan, and some tactics at our disposal. For some of our best prospects, there would be no way to even get in front of them without such a strategy or without the direct assistance of a natural partner.

The second thing we ask of natural partners is to assist in cultivation. You do not necessarily ask for this at the first skull session concerning a prospect, although you should feel comfortable in requesting this help at an early stage. Most volunteers enjoy being involved in the cultivation process, especially where it's well done. A wonderful byproduct is the fact that an excellent technique is to involve a prospect in the fund-raising process as he or she is cultivated at the same time. Many of your natural partners will also be among your 10 percent who can give 90 percent.

Finally, you may ask a natural partner to assist in solicitation, but this will come later in the process. I almost never discuss solicitation early in the strategy development stage. I seek only a cultivation plan and the involvement of the prospect.

Before Moves Management, I called the use of natural partners the centers of influence concept. I would take a friendly donor/volunteer to breakfast and ask to discuss two or three individuals. Of course, I emphasized that the information would be held in the strictest of confidence and that it would be used judiciously. I would state that we only wished to do what was appropriate with a given individual and that is why this information was vital. Once a center of influence trusted the process the information was free flowing.

Let me give you an example of the natural partner dynamic in action. For some time I had a prospect on my list for whom there was no natural partner. I asked every conceivable donor and board member without success. I finally got lucky. I needed to because this individual is frequently on the cover of *Fortune* magazine and is one of the most powerful CEOs in the country. It is not likely that I would get beyond his secretary if I were to call and seek an appointment as the friendly major gifts fund raiser from this individual's alma mater. After much searching, I found an emeritus professor who had changed this gentleman's life. Pursuant to numerous discussions, a symposium is being planned in this professor's honor. Guess who will be asked to keynote the event? It goes without saying that this would not happen unless it were an event of merit. The symposium was to be held anyway. I merely sought a name change. I should also point out that things come in bunches. Not too many weeks later I found a board member, another *Fortune* 500 CEO, who is a good professional and social friend to this gentleman. I now have a second natural partner. What is particularly nice about this additional team member is the fact that he is also a seven figure donor to our institution.

Sometimes a natural partner relationship is assumed by virtue of title or standing. For example, prospects at a certain level are worthy of presidential or board chair attention. However, the president or board chair may not even know the individual, and a part of your strategy will be to develop a natural partner relationship.

You will usually have at least one natural partner for a given prospect, but don't give up if there is no one currently to be found. If the prospect has great enough potential, you can move him or her aside and keep trying in the hope that you will secure results similar to mine.

- **Primary Player** — A primary player is the natural partner who is in the best position to advance a relationship between a given prospect and your institution. Think in terms of leverage. The primary player is the person most difficult to say no to, whether for an invitation to a cultivational event or in response to a gift solicitation. There may be more than one primary player, but you normally want to search for someone who stands out as having significant leverage. Think back to my earlier example of the *Fortune* 500 CEO. Who is more likely to be the primary player, the emeritus professor or the peer who is also a seven figure donor? There is little doubt that at critical moments, perhaps ensuring attendance at a social event or consideration of a gift, the peer CEO will be our primary player. Once again, because of title, standing or charisma you might assume that a certain volunteer or donor will become a primary player. But you may need to develop the natural partner status before that becomes possible. The primary player is the one you often think of as being involved with a gift solicitation, but we will deal with those dynamics at a later time.

- **Moves Manager** — This is the fund raiser who works with the natural partners, monitors the institution's progress with a given prospect and ensures that the organization maintains sufficient and appropriate contacts. Notice that I referred to the Moves Manager as a fund raiser. We made a mistake in this regard and learned from it. Only fund raisers should be Moves Managers, not volunteers or administrative leaders. By the way, I include administrative leaders under my umbrella term "volunteers." This is not meant in a negative sense, rather it reflects my belief that staff members who are not fund raisers need to be accorded the same treatment as our volunteers. They deserve our best efforts at educating, explaining, involving and training. In fact, the good administrative leader will begin to demand that sort of service. The mistake we made in the process of implementing Moves Management was to name one of our high level administrative leaders, someone very adroit at fund raising, as Moves Manager for one or two prospects for whom he was the key influencing individual. This person informed us that he felt this was inappropriate. He said that he expected the development professional to worry about the frequency and timing of contacts, event invitations and proposal timing. He pointed out that he was experienced and would likely amend the scenario, but he expected the development professional to prompt him about telephone calls and contacts. He promised to be a good natural partner and keep us informed, but he was not a fund raiser and did not know how to think strategically the way that development professionals must learn to do.

What are the duties of the Moves Manager concerning his or her prospects? Here's a brief job description:

- Develop a strategy for each prospect.
- Track each prospect's relationship with the organization.
- Plan contacts or moves for each prospect.
- Coordinate and prepare natural partners and primary players.
- Execute the plan. In other words, see that the contacts or moves are made.
- Reconfigure the strategy as things go along and refine the plan accordingly.
- Finally, coordinate the refined plan and execute the newly formulated moves.

The essence of the Moves Management concept is summarized in the following definition. *The process involves managing a series of steps (moves) with identified prospects (the 10 percent who can give 90 percent), the number and type of steps depending upon the individual involved, such that each prospect is moved from attention to interest to desire to action (AIDA) and then back to interest until he or she has given everything they will or can to your organization.* That definition encapsulates the life of the major gifts fund raiser. That is all I do with my professional time, with the exception of some seminars, consulting and book writing. The major gifts fund raiser is responsible for taking every prospect for whom he or she is responsible from attention to interest to desire to gift, and at that point you utilize the gift experience to cultivate for the next contribution. You do this until the individual has committed everything he or she possibly can or you realize that other organizations or alternatives are higher on the priority list. It is not a mistake that in the current $1 billion campaign, with which I am involved, a significant percentage of my donors are those who also made commitments during our last campaign. They are now giving at a higher level. Their earlier gift was used to cultivate this next gift, and they are constantly being moved through the AIDA process until it no longer makes sense to continue.

What are moves? Let's consider the following:

- *Most moves represent cultivational steps.* With the annual fund, all moves are solicitations. But in major gifts fund raising, most of our activities can be described as cultivation. Every now and then a move is a solicitation, an admittedly critical juncture which we will discuss later, but most of our contacts can be described as "mission directed" cultivation.

 - *To be effective a move must penetrate the consciousness of the prospect regarding the organization or a giving opportunity.* Alternatively, the fund raiser must learn something about the prospect and the possible giving opportunity. A potential trap, and one of the reasons cultivation has been inadequately addressed in our literature and at our seminars, is the fact that the process of cultivation is somewhat amorphous. It is easily mistaken for simple entertainment. I have heard fund raisers state that last night's move was a good one because the prospect laughed uproariously at all of the jokes and enjoyed the wine selection. That is not enough. I recall one of our staff members stating that he had made an effective move with someone because they had spent 45 minutes on the phone discussing gardening. He as an avid gardener, and when he discovered that she shared his interest the conversation was off and running. I inquired as to whether there was anything in the discussion about our organization or whether probing took place to unearth the prospect's motivational set or areas of interest. The answer was no. I pointed out that had only two or three minutes of the conversation gone like this, it could have been termed successful:

> Did you see the article in the Sunday
> supplement about Dr. Lindsey's research
> in plant pathology?
> "No, I'm sorry I missed that."
> Well, it really was fascinating. Let me send
> you a copy of the article, and if you would
> like I would enjoy arranging for a tour of
> Dr. Lindsey's lab and greenhouse.

See the difference? Our cultivation must be in accordance with a plan and be mission directed.

- *A move can be made via telephone, letter or personal visit as long as you stick to the measurements earlier described in terms of what makes a move effective.*
- *How many moves should you make?* I recommend that for your best prospects you plan one move per month, or twelve per year. Keep in mind that this can be via letter, telephone call or personal visit. I further suggest that you seek to have at least four to five of the moves accomplished through personal visit, geography permitting. We all know that the more personalized the contact the more profound the re-

sult. You may come closer to only seven to ten moves per year, but with your best prospects you should seek the more ambitious target.

If most moves are primarily cultivation, how then do you determine an objective for each discrete contact? We know what the objective is when a move is solicitation, although I will later point out that even this is more subtle than we often think it is. The cultivation moves are the tricky ones because it is not always easy to get your arms around what you want to accomplish during any given call. There are some tools we can share with you to render this process more controllable.

Some ideas borrowed from *Conceptual Selling* by Robert Miller and Steven Heiman helped me develop a framework for setting objectives for cultivational calls. Before giving you the framework, it is enlightening to review some of the traps you can fall into in this regard. As you seek to set a target for each cultivational call, you should try to avoid the following "traps."

- *Cultivational objectives that are too general.* Your goal for a given call can be so general as to be practically useless in a tactical sense. An example would be a call which is designed to "make Alice feel good about the hospital and its oncology unit." Is it important that Alice feels good about the hospital? I am sure it is, but that tells us very little about her willingness to make a major gift. We could stop people in the airport and describe the hospital's good works in 30 seconds or less and have them feel good about it. That doesn't mean they will consider a sacrificial gift. Feeling good about the hospital is no where near sufficient for a positive major gift consideration. This is just too general to be of much help.
- *Cultivational call objectives that are unrealistic.* I suppose the ultimate example of this is hoping for a gift commitment at the leadership level after the second or third move. By the way, if early in the pro-

cess your prospect commits to a major gift, and it is at the appropriate level for that individual, my recommendation is to accept and acknowledge profusely rather than state that you would prefer the prospect delay the decision because you had four or five more moves planned before solicitation! Trust me when I say that this generally does not happen in my world. I have set cultivational call objectives that are unrealistic in terms of how people operate. For instance, I have hoped for some display of enthusiasm for the idea of an endowment campaign, but even those who later made gifts didn't fall over backwards with jubilation when first presented with the concept. You have to be realistic about how people react and how long it takes for them to cross certain psychological hurdles. They may even decline your invitation to a cultivational activity two or three times before you succeed.

* *A cultivational objective that is fund raiser driven perhaps represents the trap easiest to fall into.* This type of objective is typified by a statement such as, "I am going to tell Alice about the benefits of the new oncology unit." A subtle, yet profound shift in emphasis is to seek from the call an understanding of Alice's interest in and enthusiasm for the oncology unit. You want to measure your calls by what you learn from the prospect or how the prospect reacts to a given premise, not by the volume or content of your presentation.

Keeping in mind the traps just described, an effective way to set cultivational objectives is to determine prior to each call **the best possible outcome** and **the minimum acceptable outcome**. I have had many calls where the best possible outcome was an agreement to tour the facility. The minimum acceptable outcome is that the prospect would consider a tour at a later, more convenient time. Notice that we are dealing with incrementalism. Progress is gradual. But isn't this the world we live in? Relationships are generally not built in quantum leaps. If the prospect agrees to the tour (best possible outcome) does this mean that he or she will make a gift? Of course not, but it does mean that one more positive move has been completed. What if he or she states that it is a bad time of year because of taxes, trip planning and company restructuring? Does this mean that he or she will not sometime make a major gift? Obviously not. It may just be that it is a bad time of year for them to make the tour. Your job is to ensure that a tour will be considered later (minimum acceptable outcome). Avoid quantum jumps in your conclusions. If the prospect demurs on the tour four or five times in a row, then consider that you might have a lack of interest. But proceed gradually in forming conclusions, just as our prospects proceed gradually in building relationships with us.

Perhaps one more example would help. Here I established the best possible outcome as the prospect expressing support for the aims of an endowment campaign. The minimum acceptable outcome was the willingness to receive evidence as to why we should have it. This is how prospects often think of such things and I try to formulate my objectives accordingly. During one call I had a prospect tell me that it was about time we were undertaking an endowment campaign. She observed that she had been on the museum board for years and that we were behind the times. The museum developed its endowment years ago and was now reaping the benefits. She thought that our assertive entry into this area was important and overdue. This was the best possible outcome. Did it mean she would make a major endowment gift? No, but it was clear she understood the benefits of endowment. We had made one more positive step. What about the prospect who said to me,

> I'm not even sure I understand what endowment means. I guess that's where you hold and invest the funds, although I imagine I would do a better job of investing. It's really something for you to decide. If you say it's important, then I guess it is and you should move ahead with the campaign.

Does this mean that this prospect will never make an endowment gift? I don't think it infers that at all, but it does tell us that we may need to provide some additional education in terms of the benefits, impacts and outcomes associated with endowments.

Remember that the quality of a cultivational move can generally be measured on a two point scale. The first thing to consider is the quantity and quality of the feedback received from the prospect. Of course, quality is far more important than quantity. This also points out the importance of active listening, which is a topic to be covered later in the book.

The ability to reach some degree of resolution as to the outcome or to agree upon the next step in the process is the second way to measure the quality of a cultivational call. I have discovered that it is vital to give yourself a next step with a prospect. Whether it is coming back with additional information or bringing the prospect into contact with someone else who has important information to share, you must create a reason for getting together again. This is so important that I often hold key people or relevant pieces of information in reserve. For example, I may not take a primary player on a call just so I can say to the prospect that it might be helpful or enjoyable for him or her to meet with this person. I sometimes keep data in reserve so that I am able to seek permission to come back with additional information. Having a next step, especially with your top level prospects, is vital.

To assist you in pursuing your cultivational calls, consider the following items prior to each move.

- Remind yourself of **the best possible outcome** and **the minimum acceptable outcome**.
- Review the key points to be covered during the cultivational call.
- List a small number of benefits generated by programs/projects which you believe will appeal to the prospect.
- Determine what you will ask to prospect to do, agree to or react to. In other words, determine what you

want by way of resolution or next step in the process.
cess.

- List anticipated questions and your responses to them.

Dunlop and Smith described two types of cultivational moves. The first were called foreground initiatives which are planned contacts with a specific prospect in mind. Background initiatives are group activities or services that may include one or more of your prospects. You can work both into your moves plan.

For example, you might plan to visit Denise in her office in January to talk about the oncology unit. The best possible outcome is that she accepts an invitation to tour that unit in the hospital. That is a foreground initiative and represents move number one. In February, you send Denise an article concerning the head of the oncology unit. That is a foreground initiative and move number two. In March, Denise visits the oncology unit and spends time with the doctor who heads the program. That is move number three and a foreground initiative. In April your annual founders' day dinner occurs, and you are eager to have Denise attend so that she receives positive messages about the hospital and hears the announcement of some major gifts. The message at such an event is often subtle, yet valuable. This is a background initiative and represents move number four.

Remember to leave nothing to chance when planning either foreground or background initiatives. I remember presenting at a seminar when someone inquired as to what all the circles were on my notebook page. I pointed out that this was a seating chart for an upcoming event. I very strategically placed prospects with natural partners and primary players. Of course, you want everything to be natural, not contrived. But I might go to a natural partner and point out that he or she is sitting next to a good prospect and that they might wish to inquire about the recent tour of the oncology lab. As we observed before, you really get a "big bang for the buck" this way because everyone involved in the process from natural partner to near term prospect is being cultivated.

It was at this point in our flagship seminar on major gifts fund raising that we knew we had excited fund raisers to the Moves Management concept and what it could mean to them and their organizations. Our problem was that we did not have implementation instructions. I knew what such instructions could mean because I had heard Dave Dunlop present three or four times before I finally integrated Moves Management into our operation. It took so long because I did not have a road map. Once again, we turn to Dave Dunlop and he delivers. Here is Dunlop's checklist for getting started with a Moves Management system.

1. Select 10 to 25 of your best prospects.
2. Create a file on each prospect and collect easy-to-access research. Notice the reference to easy-to-access research. One of the traps in fund raising is to fail to make the call because you are awaiting more research. I have operated under conditions where good research was almost nonexistent and in situations where it was outstanding. Frankly, my life was changed very little when conditions were improved. That is not to say that I do not value good research or use it extensively. However, you can take some additional moves to make up for a void in research data. Consider the three basic sources for research in ascending order of value. The first source is the research you obtain from objective sources as through a research department. Second up the ladder is the information you obtain from natural partners and primary players. This is more valuable because you begin to secure information about motivational triggers. At the top is the research you secure through active listening during cultivational calls. This is truly the most valuable source of information relative to the prospect and the potential giving relationship

with your institution. At this point, just insert what you have in the file and move on.

3. Identify natural partners for each prospect.

4. Consult (confidentially) with your natural partners. In other words, take your favorite natural partner to breakfast or lunch. Begin making calls on your centers of influence.

5. Preliminarily, select a primary player for each prospect. You can skip this step if you draw a complete blank, but do your best to come up with someone.

6. Preliminarily, develop a strategy for each prospect and establish gift objectives as to both amount and opportunity.

7. Plan your next five to ten moves for each prospect.

8. Implement the moves for each prospect, and after each move we recommend you do the following:
    - Review and record what has transpired. Do your call reports, however brief.
    - Refine your strategy and gift objectives as appropriate. You will not often need to make these revisions, but every now and then it is called for. We simply want you to consider if you still feel comfortable with your preliminary gift objective after each call. Occasionally you will run into a situation such as what I experienced with the gentleman who could see no need to support faculty.
    - Fine tune the planning for your next move. The reason I want you to consider the next move immediately is that the information from the call just made will be fresh in your mind. You may have heard something that will help you with your next step. For example, the prospect may have mentioned that he has a high regard for one of your board members, and perhaps you will decide to invite that person to the cultivation activity.

Why do I qualify 5 and 6 with the word preliminarily? This is because we want you to undertake these steps even though we know the decisions you make early on may change as you move through the process. They may even change many times. However, it is human nature to have difficulty when there are too many possibilities to address. Even if you later revise your choices, preliminary selection of a primary player and a gift objective provides you with something to measure against. For example, I was measuring against a primary player during a call when the prospect stated that he respected this individual but found him to be too academic and obtuse. This is a natural type of occurrence in human affairs, but at that point I decided to change my primary player. Another instance I remember is one where I had targeted someone for an endowed chair. I measured against this by referencing the endowed chair that was established by one of this prospect's friends. He remarked that it was a wonderful and generous gift, but he was surprised his friend would support faculty. After all, there are many eccentric faculty members and he worried about there being a lot of "dead wood" because of tenure. Needless to say, I decided to develop another opportunity rather than focus on faculty support through an endowed chair. This is why we want you to preliminarily make these choices and be prepared to change as you measure against the scenario you envision.

9. At year end, or the beginning of the year if it is more convenient, review the status of each prospect, refine your strategy and objectives, and plan the next five to ten moves. When planning your moves you can use a calendar charting system, an automatic tickler system, your personal calendar, or whatever method works the best for you.

10. At year end or the beginning of the year, add and delete prospects from your list as appropriate.

It should be emphasized that the Moves Management system is just as applicable to the small or one person shop as it is to the large operation. In fact, it may even be easier to implement in the small operation. Were I functioning as a one person department I would surely use Moves Management with the index card and calendar system of old. If you are in a rather large operation you should not let the extensive "base touching" and coordination needs thwart your efforts. It can be done, as I've discovered through my own experience. Implementing Moves Management and overcoming turf sensitivities was a little bit like processing orange juice. It wasn't pretty, but the outcome was fine. All of these comments are simply my way of urging you to avoid delay in employing this useful concept in your daily life as a major gifts fund raiser. Even if your organization fails to adopt the concept, you can utilize it and its strategic implications with your particular prospects and donors.

You will note that we suggest you start by selecting 10 to 25 of your best prospects. We wanted to make the number modest so that the small shop, or the isolated person in the big operation, would not be intimidated. It is also true that many fund raisers wear more than one hat for an organization or department. We want this to be realistic, and we want nothing to stand in the way of implementation.

Someone who had attended a few of my training sessions and was president of a local chapter of a large organization approached me after one of my seminars. She confessed that when she implemented Moves Management she cut the number of prospects to five. After all, she wore several hats and was CEO of that very small unit. She indicated that for the first time in its history the program had received a six figure gift, and it was attributable to the Moves Management methodology. She observed that she has now added another 15 or 20 prospects to her list and had given up some of her other duties. Moves Management had paid handsome dividends and the organization longed for more gifts. As success is secured in major gifts fund raising, organizations begin to recognize the disproportionate impact of large gifts. The result is that you will be called upon to do all that is necessary to increase the time spent in this arena, and the number of prospects you handle will surely grow.

The question is begged. How many prospects can you reasonably handle? We have polled fund raisers over the years concerning this very issue. Here is the consensus. If all you do full-time is major gifts fund raising, then you can probably handle 100 reasonably well. Perhaps 50 would be ideal, but 100 is reasonable. This is especially so given the fact that many under your purview may be in a stewardship or maintenance mode, which requires fewer moves than is true for those close to the major gift decision. If you are with a big organization, you will probably end up with 200 or more prospects, and this will be more than you can efficiently handle. I have been saved by a marvelous staff who make many moves on my behalf.

It should never be assumed that Moves Management applies only to mega gift prospects. Very often those examples are utilized simply because they are dramatic and interesting. The concept works equally well at lower gift magnitudes. For instance, when I am pursuing the possibility of a modest bequest from a retired faculty member, I consult with other retired faculty members (i.e., natural partners) and hopefully uncover someone who might state the case with greater credibility and leverage (i.e., primary player). Once again, don't let assumptions about applications different from yours hold you back from implementing. Any time personalized relationship building is merited with a given prospect, then the Moves Management concept should be utilized.

To assist you in dealing with your prospects, especially when the number burgeons, it is useful to have some sort of classification system. Dave Dunlop developed an interesting approach in that regard. Dunlop likes to classify his prospects as follows:

- Those ready to make a major gift.

- Those needing some cultivation but who would consider a major gift in the near future.
- Those needing extensive cultivation.
- Those with capability, but little or no reason to give.

Dunlop's typology is a useful way to consider your time management. It goes without saying that you must focus your greatest effort on those prospects closest to the major gift decision and with the greatest capability. You don't judge them to be better human beings, but from a business and fund-raising standpoint you must go first to those who can have the greatest impact. For many organizations new to major gifts fund raising, there may not be any prospects in the top category or two. For all of us, even the mature programs, the greatest number will reside in the classification of those need-ing extensive cultivation. The point is that you need to spend time with the 10 percent who can give 90 percent, and indeed the correct 10 percent, and the prospect grid and the above method of classification will help you make those decisions.

A more precise method of classifying prospects, but one which is compatible with the Dunlop methodology, is noted below. This system is amenable to incorporation into tracking systems and, therefore, is convenient for many. However, it is a useful way to consider your prospects, whether you are highly automated or not. The two ways of classification combine giving potential with stage in the process from a tactical stand-point. You should modify this to match your particular needs. Certainly, you will likely want to change the dollar amounts. It matters not the various levels from an absolute dollar stand-point. What is important is that those levels reflect your fund raising situation. With that in mind, I offer the following pos-sibility.

Long-term giving potential	Status
1 - $1 million or above	A Solicit.
2 - $750,000 to $1 million	B Cultivate.
3 - $500,000 to $750,000	C Qualify.
4 - $250,000 to $500,000	D Stewardship.
5 - $100,000 to $250,000	E Inactive.
6 - $50,000 to $100,000	
7 - $25,000 to $50,000	

I urge you to adapt and most importantly implement the Moves Management concept. Call it whatever you will, but you need to get it under way if you are to maximize the potential for your organization. Nightingale said that success is " . . the progressive realization of a worthwhile goal or idea." The organization you represent has a worthwhile and important mission, and the dollars you raise are vital to its progressive realization. It is imperative that you put forth the very finest major gift program possible, and Moves Management will help you accomplish that.

7

Determinants of Success in Asking for the Gift

In major gifts fund raising, cultivational calls, where you listen and nurture, far outnumber solicitation calls. The ratio of one to the other depends upon the particular prospect, his or her relationship with the organization, and the level of the solicitation. But whatever the specifics, it is safe to say that time spent in cultivation outweighs that expended on solicitation. Eventually, however, you need to ask your prospect for a gift. It's what we so often think of as fund raising, and we all worry about it. The good news is that there is much we can do to improve our performance.

I am a strong believer in nonmanipulative fund raising. I don't want to manipulate people. If you truly love people, why would you want to manipulate them? Further, I'm certainly not smart enough to manipulate people. Because of my belief system in this regard, the tips, techniques and methodologies I share with you should be adapted to your natural style of doing things. They are designed to aid in communications, ensure maximum understanding and enhance the opportunity for success. Manipulative they are not.

It is important that we never forget what our donors want out of the giving relationship. Whether it be prestigious association, feeling good about oneself, recognition or memorializing a loved one, our job is to demonstrate to donors how a gift to our institution will satisfy those aims.

I call what is sought from the giving relationship a donor's "concept." This is an idea that is lifted from *Conceptual Selling* by Miller and Heiman. It is vital to remember that in any given solicitation scenario people donate for their reasons, not ours. Donating is really a special case of decision making, and such decision making, as we earlier observed, is sequential. The donating decision is made in a series of predictable and logical steps. By following the prospect's sequence you find that either there is a fit with that prospect and your giving opportunity, which leads to a gift, or there is no such fit, at least for now. Of one thing I can assure you, by ignoring the prospect's decision making process, and what he or she wants from the giving relationship, you will surely lose the gift.

When considering gift solicitation it is again useful to start from the general and narrow to the specific. There are several key determinants of our success, or lack thereof, in asking for a contribution. It may sound like journalism theory, but whether or not you succeed in securing a major gift will depend upon **who** asks for it; for **what** are you asking; **how much** are you asking for; **where** are you asking; and **when** will you ask. These are the key strategic decisions you must make, and the building blocks for those decisions are the pieces of information you secure during the cultivation process. Throughout your cultivation activities you are attempting to decide upon the solicitor, the gift target and opportunity, the time of asking and the location for same. Each of these factors merits independent discussion.

Who? We know that who asks for the gift is a key variable. In fact, our donors tell us this. Certainly, we can all recognize that nothing is more effective than a peer-to-peer solicitation, the solicitor having already committed an appropriate sum. This represents the situation with maximum leverage. It is most difficult to say no to a friend/peer who has made a commitment as sacrificial as the one being sought. However, it is a challenge to create this solicitation scenario consistently, and, indeed, it may only be possible in a minority of cases. Let us all recognize at the start that maximum leverage is not often required for the annual fund renewal or upgrade, nor is it always vital at or below the "stop and think" major gift level. The more you ask for the more important any one of the key determinants becomes. For example, I do not need our high powered campaign chair to secure an annual fund renewal from a prospect, but I surely need that sort of clout when seeking a leadership commitment beyond anything the prospect has donated before.

Why is the peer solicitation scenario not always attainable? Here are three fundamental reasons you may not be able to create this context:

1. *Your chosen primary player may not like asking for a gift.* He or she may simply refuse to do so.
2. *Your chosen peer solicitor may not be very good at it.* (By the way, I classify administrative leaders as volunteers in terms of how we prepare and utilize their talents. The only difference is that there is not the same giving expectation attached to an administrative leader as there is to a peer solicitor.) The plain fact of the matter is that sometimes the person who would be best in terms of leverage is a poor solicitor. It never ceases to amaze me how many high powered decision makers have a hard time with a gift solicitation. I remember one solicitor who somehow could never utter the amount of the expected commitment. You will hear later that asking for a specific amount, and specific purpose, in clear and concise terms, is important. This volunteer just couldn't handle it. He would push the proposal across the table and utter something like "We know you will do everything you can to help us." I used to go along on the solicitation so that I could add clarification and ensure that the request was clear. I remember another volunteer who, despite extensive training, would ramble and obfuscate the discussion to the extent that I couldn't even decipher our purpose. You do

not use a volunteer who is inept at solicitation. Let me tell you about a kind and devoted volunteer — a primary player on our faculty — who proved not to be effective his first time out. We were soliciting a $1.5 million gift from an entrepreneur/corporate captain. We were having breakfast in a mahogany-lined boardroom while the prospect's helicopter awaited his departure some 30 minutes hence. The primary player was key — the likely reason for a gift to my institution — and I had scripted him carefully. Unfortunately, this was his first experience and he "choked," as the saying goes. His opening statement — at great variance from my recommendation — was as follows: "Mr. Sturtevant has something important to ask you," at which time I gasped and fearlessly charged ahead. The lesson: Know thy volunteer and plan accordingly. By the way, we still got the gift.

3. *Your volunteer may be giving below capability.* This is important. There are few inviolate rules in major gifts fund raising. After all, it is far more of an art than a science. However, one verity that comes close to inviolate is that of never having someone solicit a peer if he or she is giving below capability. It sends the wrong message and prospects scale off of what the solicitor has done. And believe me, prospects somehow find out what others have done. It is far better to have staff solicit the gift without volunteer assistance than to send someone in who is giving below capability. In fact, our donors are very clear in sending that message.

In the Tobin survey cited earlier, philanthropists were asked what makes for an effective solicitor. They cited three attributes, two of which are probably not surprising. An effective solicitor was deemed to be someone who possessed knowledge, demonstrated commitment and exuded passion. The reference to passion is interesting given the fact that many of these philanthropists were sophisticated and well entrenched in the conservative establishment. It just goes to show you that true belief is an effective sales tool. The commitment reference is also of interest. Our philanthropists told us that they were singularly unimpressed with people asking them for a gift who were giving below capability. The philanthropists indicated that they would rather have a staff member seek the gift than a peer who contributes less than sacrificially. These philanthropists were clear in pointing out that it was not necessary for a solicitor to give at the same level as they were being asked to consider. However, the giving level for the solicitor must be appropriate to his or her capacity. That also means it is important for administrative leaders and for development professionals to be giving, regardless of level. The precise level is not important in these cases, but the act of participation, perhaps the passion demonstrated by giving, does send an important message.

What and for how much? I offer these together because the same overarching principle applies. I speak here of specificity. It is strongly recommended that you ask for a specific amount for a specific purpose. You need to be as specific as possible. Have I ever dealt with ranges or project lists in my solicitations? Yes, but I resist it to the extent possible. It may not be critical at lower levels of giving, but where major gifts are involved, specificity is to be strongly preferred. Prospects respond best to precise, concise solicitations. As we will later see, precision and specificity are also vital because psychologists tell us that where confusion exists a decision maker demurs. Too many options, whether giving levels or opportunities, leads to confusion. If you are not quite positive about how much to ask for and for what, consider a preproposal cultivational call. I have used this tool extensively. This is where you visit a prospect and in essence convey the message that the current meeting is not for the purpose of soliciting a gift. I often state that I intend to arrange for a return visit at which time we will discuss the prospect's role in our effort or opportunity. This visit, however, is designed to discuss where we are and to explore preliminarily the prospect's degree of understanding, interest and enthusiasm. You are probing the prospect's feelings to ensure accuracy. One way to do this is by talking about what others have chosen to do with their support. A good example of a pre-proposal cultivation call is provided by a solicitation effort I was involved with a few years ago. Our primary player, who happened to be the university president, indicated that following his last visit with our prospect he became concerned we were seeking funding for the wrong opportunity. We were about to propose an endowment gift, when our president's instincts told him that bricks and mortar were of greater interest. We agreed that I would do a pre-proposal cultivational call. I told the prospect that he was important to the president, and as a reflection of that esteem the president wanted to personally discuss the prospect's role in our campaign. I stated that the president was looking forward to visiting with him in the near future for this purpose. As an aside, I stated that in their last meeting the president sensed as much enthusiasm about building opportunities in our campaign as with endowment. The prospect became animated and his eyes lit up. He said,

> No one really knows what an endowed chair is or who the person was who funded it. But a building is something you can see and feel. When you have your name on a building, it really says something. And it is long lasting.

Our prospect told us all that we needed to know. As of this writing, a building gift from this wonderful human being is in the finalization stage.

Where? A good rule of thumb to follow is that the prospect should be solicited where he or she is most comfortable. This probably means his or her turf. The fundamental reason for this is that people are most amenable to a positive decision when they are most comfortable. This represents a bit of a conundrum because both you and the prospect are nervous. Nevertheless, the principle is a sound one. Psychologists teach us that prospects will demure or defer a decision if their level of discomfort is too high. There are ways to help a prospect feel comfortable other than location, and these will be explored later. For now, the basic premise to recognize is that you want an environment which is conducive to consideration. This does not mean that you should never solicit a prospect at your facility. It simply means that you need to be sensitive to this issue. Some fund raisers have a principle that they will never solicit a gift in a restaurant. This is not a hard and fast rule with me. I have had many effective solicitations over a meal, but I am careful with the staging and timing. You certainly do not want the critical question interrupted by an inquiry as to your desire for more coffee. Private club settings can be especially effective because you can set the stage for comfort while controlling the flow of activity. One of our seminar attendees told me of a solicitation she orchestrated in a restaurant. She was concerned that her hard charging volunteer would not follow the script which called for solicitation only after the meal was completed and there was no danger of interruption. She arrived at the restaurant early and told the waiter to quickly attend to the drink order. She further instructed him to avoid returning to the table, under the threat of physical harm, until he was signaled by her. Sure enough, immediately following the delivery of the drinks the board chair started in by saying something like, "Let's not beat around the bush. Here's what we want to discuss with you . . ." Our colleague knew her volunteer. Incidentally, the solicitation was successful.

When? The solicitation should occur when you feel the timing is appropriate. That's right, trust your instincts. They will serve you well. If you are uncertain, then try a pre-proposal cultivational call. You will come to trust your visceral feelings. Through experience and training your judgments will be well honed. Just so long as you have had a reasonable amount of cultivation, you will probably not harm your position even if your solicitation is a little bit premature. We should also recognize that timing is not quite as critical at less sacrificial levels of giving or when the solicitation is well below what the prospect has earlier done with other charitable causes.

I am often asked by fund-raising colleagues about my method for determining precisely how much to ask for. One heuristic which is extremely helpful is the prospect's largest single gift to any charitable organization. If you feel your organization's position is stronger, you can exceed that amount with some degree of confidence. On the other hand, if you realistically believe you are down the list of priorities for this individual, you will need to scale down the solicitation target. However, we always want to be bold in this regard. Asking a natural partner can be very revealing, although peers have a tendency to discount what friends will do. You approach volunteers by informing them of the confidentiality of the inquiry and of your simple desire to ensure that what the organization does with the prospect is appropriate. I have below noted a chart relative to the amount of the ask which was put forth by one of our colleagues:

Gift Over Time	Income	% of Income	Net Worth	% of Net Worth
$ 25,000	$100,000	25%	$500,000	5%
50,000	250,000	20%	500,000	10%
100,000	250,000	40%	1,000,000	10%
500,000	500,000	100%	5,000,000	10%
1,000,000	500,000	200%	10,000,000	10%

I sometimes hesitate to use the chart because it is dangerous to interpret the guidelines literally. Note that some solicitations equal or exceed annual income. Is this realistic? Sure it is. This could certainly be true where your prospect is giving out of capital. Also, keep in mind that we are talking about a gift over time. You will note that the chart indicates a solicitation should never exceed 10 percent of net worth, and I would concur that at any given time that is a useful outside limit. Five percent may even be more realistic.

Whatever the preliminary gift target based on the chart and the other factors noted above, I always modify my answer by such things as the stage in the life cycle of the donor; the donor's ability to replace assets; prior involvement with and support of my institution; and prior philanthropic experience.

Finally, just use your judgment. If the largest single gift to your organization is $1,000, then a $1 million gift may be an unrealistic quantum leap. It is better to have the donor enjoy a good giving experience at a lower level before you begin making jumps which reflect the multiplication table. I have learned that you can solicit the next gift much sooner than anticipated, even sometimes returning during the initial pledge period or prior to a campaign's finish. I have also observed that the greater the gap between the last contribution and a level considered sacrificial, the sooner you can return with another opportunity.

I have some rules of thumb or tips about personal solicitation that I have found useful. I offer these in no particular order and urge your additions. These are helpful reminders and suggestions.

- *Prior to a solicitation, remind yourself that each one of your prospects is unique in what he or she seeks from the giving relationship.* Each is also unique in terms of emphasis on values and how he or she wishes to make an impact in this world. Be sure to reflect that unique mindset in your approach, proposal and script.
- *Prior to a solicitation, remind yourself that your prospect is busy and his or her time is important.* Individuals respond best to honest, direct, concise and precise approaches. Does your approach fit those guidelines?
- *Before soliciting a gift, remind yourself that donors are not under any obligation to give and be sure than any such message is expunged from your script and proposal.*
- *Remember that prospects give to well managed organizations whose aspirations they share, not to needy causes.* Will your organization's efficiency and effectiveness be reflected in your solicitation proposal? Are your prepared to prove why your organization is the very best in which to make an investment to further a shared dream?

- *It is important to establish a confident and friendly atmosphere in your solicitation setting if you are to maximize your opportunity for success.* Once again, we have a conundrum. How can you establish a confident and friendly atmosphere when all of the parties involved are nervous? Experience certainly helps. So does the next item, which I have purposely coupled with this admonition.

- *Rehearse and visualize prior to your solicitation.* Later in the book I will provide you with a marvelous framework for scripting a solicitation. I used to prepare a memo for the solicitation team in which I would recount the history of the relationship between the prospect and the organization. Further, I would outline what we were seeking and describe the roles to be played by the various solicitation team members. I would indicate anticipated questions and reflect on who should respond and in what manner. Now I utilize the framework I will describe later. The point to be made here is that preparation is vital. I often avoided such preparation because I was concerned about the valuable time of our volunteers and felt they surely would not wish to sit still for some sort of rehearsal. I was wrong. Tobin's research revealed that donors felt inadequately prepared for solicitations and that they wanted the charitable organizations with which they were associated to do a better job of training them. I never like to ask for extra time from busy volunteers, especially those making million dollar decisions which affect thousands of lives, but when I asked many of them if they would find it helpful to receive training they responded affirmatively and enthusiastically. After all, they have no reason to feel comfortable as fund raisers, and many are used to being well prepared by staff members for those activities carried out in their business. We found that even the volunteers at the highest levels of potential were very pleased to receive training and participate in such activities as role playing. At the very least, plan to gather your team 20 to 30 minutes prior to a solicitation, perhaps over a cup of coffee near where you are meeting the prospect, to review everything before the call. Things will go more smoothly and your volunteers will appreciate your professionalism. Trust me, your volunteers will welcome this sort of preparation. In fact, many of our experienced volunteers now demand to know when they can get together with us prior to a solicitation for a preparation discussion.

- *Build questions into your solicitation.* When I provide you with your scripting mechanism, I will indicate where it is convenient to insert questions. At this juncture, I just want to establish the premise that participation on the part of the prospect is vital.

- *During cultivational calls you should be talking only about 30 to 40 percent of the time, with 60 to 70 percent reserved for the prospect. The nature of a solicitation move is such that it will likely be closer to 70 percent talking on the part of the solicitation team, but you must do the best you can to encourage the involvement of your prospect.* Asking questions is one way to accomplish that. It is not necessary that the questions be profound, a simple nodding of the head will suffice. I sometimes ask prospects questions the answers to which I already know, just to get them responding. It's that important.

- *Build an indication of the form of recognition into your solicitation.* A few prospects truly seek anonymity, but these are far fewer than those who say they do. You will not offend someone who truly wishes anonymity by mentioning recognition because you can always indicate that, of course, his or her wishes will prevail. You can assure her that your organization will honor the request for anonymity but you mentioned recognition simply because you want her to know of your sincere gratitude for the consideration. You will not hurt yourself. Some prospects have recognition at the top of their list, and they may be the easiest to deal with. For most of us, it is somewhere on the list. If it is not a primary motivation, it certainly is a "feel good" consideration. It is important to mention it. It is also true that for many it is far more important than they will ever let on, and you hurt your case if recognition is not discussed.

- *Maintain your optimism and enthusiasm no matter how you think the solicitation is going.* I have found that in many cases it is easy to misread how the prospect is reacting, especially given the natural tension of such a situation. Enthusiasm and optimism are infectious, and it is important that you maintain this energy. Experience has taught me not to draw conclusions prematurely or read too much into any given reaction. I have secured many gift commitments when I thought the level of enthusiasm was low or the concerns about the opportunity were high. Keep the solicitation upbeat!

- *Don't go too soon to the gift spread or the deferred gift options.* There are a few reasons why I say this. First, these options may not answer your prospect's particular concern. Sometimes the prospect is not even sure why he or she has some reservations or negative reactions. A bit of probing is better than jumping to an assumed solution. Second, it is always nice to have some ammunition in reserve. If the prospect expresses price resistance two or three times, it's nice to be able to offer the option of spreading the gift over several years. By the time you utilize that option you are certain that it is a solution to the true problem, and at that point you are making the gift decision much easier for the individual involved. You should even be more reluctant to jump to the deferred gift solution. Certainly, with a building project a deferred gift presents a problem. But even where endowment is involved, there is no reason to mention this option too soon. Once again, it is good to have a "trump card" in reserve should you need it at a later time. With the deferred gift option, I usually pull it out only after several attempts at more current alternatives. I have witnessed volunteers receiving price resistance during a solicitation immediately mention that with endowment an estate plan provision works very nicely. By being so premature you may encourage a deferred gift where one would not have otherwise been necessary. You also preclude the use of a tool which can be effectively utilized at a later time.

- *Don't discount the gift target too soon.* When you are seeking leadership or sacrificial gifts you can expect some price resistance. You should avoid the temptation to react by trying a lower amount or asking the prospect to define what seems reasonable. I have two reasons for saying this. One reason is that I have found things have a way of changing over time. I recall a prospect indicating that he thought we were somewhat daft for asking at such a high level. "Crazy" may have been the chosen term. Surprisingly enough, after a weekend of consideration the prospect said, "I still think you're crazy, but I've thought about it and there may be a way to get this thing done." Give the prospect time to consider everything. You may preclude a gift at the original level by discounting too soon. To coin a Sy Seymour phrase, "a cucumber needs to soak before it becomes a pickle." The second reason to avoid discounting is that it just does not look very professional. It is better to come back another day with another option. To discount too soon makes it look as if you are on a fishing expedition and that you are a price haggler. Obviously, if the prospect is adamant and very clear you may have no choice but to look at other options at a lower giving level, but this should be avoided where possible. It is far better to come back another day to discuss other exciting opportunities when it becomes clear that the original proposal won't fly.

• *Welcome objections.* In a later chapter we will discuss why objections are really very helpful and how you can respond to them.

Our organizations will secure major gifts even if we do it all wrong by ignoring the general precepts just discussed. We will even secure gifts if we fail to ask. This is because our organizations are important and touch many lives. People will step forward with major support because our organizations have made a difference to them. It is just that we can be more successful if we employ certain techniques and live according to certain principles. That is the justification for this book.

I like to tell groups that we will secure major gifts perhaps 20 percent of the time simply because our organizations serve important ends. This could be considered the receipt of gifts "over the transom." We would like to do much better than that, which is why we attend seminars and read books on fund raising. We can, perhaps, be 80 percent successful in our major gift solicitation efforts if we are truly committed and effective. We will never be 100 percent successful just because of the nature of the process. It is a people business which is subject to numerous influencing factors. Things happen, and we never secure 100 percent of the gifts we seek. The 20 percent/80 percent measurements are not intended to be precise. It really could be 10 percent and 90 percent. The concept of importance is that certain factors play a key role in how successful we really are. This is how I developed my success continuum. Take a look at it in chart form.

Success Continuum

20% Success		80% Success
Ask	Cultivation and Solicitation Method	Listen
Money	Donor Orientation	Values
Little	Degree or Deliberation	Great
	Life Cycle Stage	
Survival	Accumulation	Distribution
Young	Age Line	Less Young

In terms of the cultivation and solicitation method, we are far less successful when we are in the asking mode and more successful when we are active and effective listeners. I know that this observation sounds simplistic, even trite. It also happens to be true. This explains why later in this book I have devoted so much attention to active listening for fund raisers.

In terms of donor orientation, if we view our prospects simply as sources of funds we will be far less successful than if we seek shared values. People stretch to the farthest limits of that which they are capable when the giving opportunity expresses values important to them. Gift opportunities need to be reflective of how prospects wish to be remembered in life. It is their legacy, if you will. When you seek to understand a prospect's shared values and link that with the opportunity at your institution, you maximize your chances for success. Notice how nicely it ties together with active listening. You learn of shared values through the listening process. If you simply view people as a source of funds, perhaps you are burned out or not suited for the development profession. Try to match your prospect's values to your institutional opportunities. The result will be stretch gifts of profound impact.

Degree of deliberation is an interesting consideration. What I really mean here is that I find people tendering more profound expressions of support the more involved they feel in the development of the concept. If you make prospects feel a part of the creation and crafting of the outcome, you increase your chances for success. The need or opportunity may be preexisting, but this type of deliberation should become a part of the cultivation, involvement and solicitation process.

Life cycle stage and the age line should really be taken together. They are loosely related. In terms of life cycle we go through three basic stages. We will ignore the survival stage because a prospect at this point on the continuum will not likely grade out on our prospect grid. Many of us remember survival from college days when we were uncertain as to where the next meal would come from. Most of us go through an extended accumulation stage, loosely related to age, and at a certain point in our lives we become far more amenable to the consideration of a major release of assets for a gift. Some of us may never reach the distribution stage. The life cycle stage and the age lines are not factors which you can influence. You can only recognize them, but the concept is important because you are likely to confront them. Accumulation is particularly acute among those who have been affected by a depression or a major reversal. Entrepreneurs are also oriented toward accumulation. With some donors I have witnessed a conversion seemingly over night from accumulation to distribution. They indicate that they weren't ready when we first discussed the opportunity, but they would like to revisit the possibilities again. Sometimes continuity is the key to your success. Just being there when the donor is ready to talk.

Let me give you some examples of accumulation. I know of a gentleman who could write a check to our organization for $1 million. It would not be difficult for him. However, he is so focused on buying and building companies, perhaps in quest of the *Forbes* 400, that he would never consider doing this. He has even admitted to me that someday he would like to make a major gift, but it is too difficult now because he is continually making acquisitions. Over breakfast he told me that one day he would make the seven figure contribution he knows we want, and my only observation was that I hoped we were having coffee together when that moment came. There is not a lot I can do to "sell around" the accumulation psychology. I have found it effective to secure below "stop and think" gifts from these donors and use those gifts to give them great satisfaction. You can continue to raise the bar over time. The idea is to expand their sights and simply to be there when the distribution phase arrives.

I remember another incident which reflects a form of accumulation versus distribution. I had worked with a couple for several years and everything about the gift opportunity and our approach seemed perfect. We had the right opportunity, the right amount and the right primary player. We somehow could not get over the line with this lovely couple. Finally, I asked the husband if he was afraid of losing everything. We had the kind of relationship where I could make such a query. He said that he had this fear because he had seen fortunes dissipated almost overnight. He told me of his vivid memory of a soup can on the kitchen table and how difficult it was to decide whether or not to open it. If the two of them had the soup that evening, perhaps there wouldn't be anything tomorrow. This was during the depression, and it is understandable that he never forgot the experience. He had strong donative intent, but it scared him to think of releasing assets when he might need them for personal purposes. This was a couple with a net worth of about $30 million! I pointed out that when they "went down the tubes" the rest of us would be down there with arms outstretched to catch them. He knew that intellectually. It's just that he couldn't overcome the psychology. There was nothing I could do about it directly, but we succeeded in going to the deferred gift option. This way the assets would be there if they were needed, but they would support the cause they loved to the extent they remained. He even asked me to tell the president that they would work hard to preserve all of the assets because they truly wanted the project to be funded.

Be on the lookout for life cycle stage because you will surely confront it in your major gifts fund-raising career.

Robert Cialdini of Arizona State University is a psychologist who has done a lot of research pertaining to how people make yes or no decisions. He has applied this research to the realm of fund raising, and he has even done some work with the Arizona State University fund-raising staff. His book, *Influence*, is fascinating.

Cialdini enumerates six principles of influence which are useful to fund raisers considering the solicitation dynamic. Cialdini's six principles, and some of the implications, are as follows:

- *Reciprocity is the obligation you feel to return the form of behavior you receive.* This is why it is effective in fund raising to point to services, satisfactions, and benefits your organization has provided in the past. You can also seek to actively generate benefits, and ensure that they are recognized by your prospects, so that support flows in return.

- *We conform to the recommendations of appropriate authority figures.* This relates to the use of leverage in solicitations. This is called the authority principle.

- *Commitment means that after we assume a position we try to act in ways that fit what we've already done or said.* Inertia would be the term in physics. We all seek consistency. Therefore, establishing involvement (commitment) before making the ask is essential. The gift must conform to a belief or a position already assumed.

- *Using the belief, attitudes and actions of those around us to determine our own (e.g. using lists of previous donors) reflects the consensus principle.*

- *One of Cialdini's more interesting principles is that of scarcity.* He found that as opportunities become scarce we perceive them to be more valuable. This means that we should stress the uncommon or unique features of our organization, service, opportunity or giving experience. We must differentiate giving opportunities, even if only by the name carried on an unrestricted endowment fund, so that our prospects view what we are asking them to do as important and urgent.

- *It will come as no surprise that Cialdini found a friendship/liking dynamic.* That is, people prefer to comply with the requests of others whom they know and like. Cialdini's research indicates that the most effective way to get a "yes" often has nothing to do with the request itself. Rather, the psychological context (e.g. who was asking) is often the critical factor.

Finally, we can again borrow from *Conceptual Selling* and remind ourselves of some important donor perspectives which can arise during gift solicitation. There are some basic issues which exist for our prospects, and they can preclude the positive decision if the gift is viewed as a negative influence on one or more of them. The prospect may decline a gift opportunity if he or she is concerned about any of the following.

- Loss of power
- Loss of control
- Loss of recognition
- Loss of flexibility
- Loss of security

Obviously, many are interrelated. My friend who had vivid memories of the depression worried about loss of flexibility, security and control. It is vital that we probe to understand our donors' concerns and seek to ameliorate them. We must demonstrate how our opportunity will provide satisfaction which far outweighs any potential negative.

We should always remember that by soliciting a gift we are giving people an opportunity to secure satisfaction they can gain in no other fashion. I have observed this to be the case, and it is important that we believe it. It is also essential that we reflect that principle in our discussions and proposals. Thoreau said that "To affect the quality of the day, that is the highest of the arts." In soliciting gifts, we must show our donors how their generosity will affect the quality of the day for generations to come.

8

The Ultimate Move — Making the Ask — How to Prepare and Respond

It should be apparent by now that I am a firm believer in preparation when it comes to gift solicitation. There is no bigger favor you can do for yourself than to adequately prepare for the solicitation call. Our donors agree. Tobin's Jewish philanthropists observed that they felt inadequately prepared by the charitable organizations for which they were asked to play the role of solicitor. They thought that some sort of mentoring or training system would be of value. It is up to the development professional to ensure adequate preparation for the solicitation team, whether in the context of an annual campaign or a mega gift opportunity.

I used to prepare for gift solicitation by way of a memorandum which was disseminated to the solicitation team. This missive would start by recounting the history of the relationship between the prospect and my organization. I would describe areas of prior involvement and the relationships which existed between natural partners and the prospect. I would also summarize the giving history, emphasizing outcomes and perceived donor satisfactions. My memorandum would then launch into a description of the call at hand and what I expected. I would discuss what should be presented and the role to be played by respective members of the solicitation team. I would raise possible objections and responses, with a notation of who on our team should handle a given question or observation.

The memorandum was a most valuable tool. I would submit it to members of the solicitation team, either in advance of or as a part of our preparation meeting. As noted earlier, it is mandatory to arrange for a preparation meeting even if it is only minutes prior to the actual call. I only abandoned the memorandum approach when I found something better. Indeed, there is a far better tool, perhaps one of the most valuable I have come across in my fund-raising career, and I'm eager to share it with you.

Aryeh Nesher is an experienced fund raiser. As experienced as they come. Nesher was sent to this country by Golda Meir to raise money for Israel. His approach, fashioned by a different era and somewhat unique market dynamics, is much different from mine, but he has great wisdom to share with us. It was during one of our seminars that I observed his presentation of an anatomy of the gift solicitation. It is an incredibly useful framework for scripting the solicitation.

I will present Nesher's framework in outline form. I have found this format to be useful because you can expand or contract the subheadings depending upon the experience of the solicitation team, the complexity of the gift scenario and the magnitude of the ask. You can also put the initials of members of the solicitation team next to those items each person is to handle. It is a marvelously concise and logical way to script the gift solicitation.

Nesher had four sections to his outline. I have added a fifth. Nesher's framework started with the opening or introduction, but I thought it was important to formally acknowledge what I call the preliminaries. Some explanation might prove of value.

I recommend that you script your solicitation, beginning with the opening or introduction, for 15 to 20 minutes. The former would be best, but you certainly do not want to script a solicitation for longer than 20 minutes. You will not hold your prospect's attention for any longer, and we know that prospects respond best to concise, precise gift requests. We fully understand that the solicitation may take hours and may even occur over more than one call. That will be because of the circumstance or at the donor's behest. We still want you to script your solicitation for 15 to 20 minutes because that will force your back to a consistent and recurring theme. A little redundancy regarding key points and benefits is never harmful.

Preliminaries are dictated by the personality of the particular prospect. Those of us who deal disproportionately with typical planned gift prospects are used to preliminaries which take an hour or more. It is important to ask about the antiques, grandchildren and world cruise. With some of my prospects, the preliminaries are extremely brief. A question about the family, business or golf game will suffice and then it is time to move on. I even have a prospect who looks at his watch when we enter the office, and I do not need a course on fund raising to tell me that we should get right to the bottom line with this gentleman. Under preliminaries on your outline you can make helpful notations concerning areas about which inquiries need to be made. The opening or introduction is typified by a statement such as "We're here today to talk to you about...." That is when the stop watch is punched, and you need to script for 15 to 20 minutes from that point forward.

Let's look at Nesher's outline, a framework aptly called "The Anatomy of an Ask."

I. PRELIMINARIES

Know thy prospect. The preliminaries are as appropriate to the particular personality. In this section you can note areas of importance to your prospect about which inquiries should be made.

II. OPENING OR INTRODUCTION

The opening or introduction is where the hourglass gets turned over, and from this point forward the script should be tailored for a 15 to 20 minute solicitation.

- A key objective during this phase is to gain the attention of your prospect. Some fund raisers believe the best way to do this is by indicating the level of the sought for gift. The idea is to present a premise much like,

  > We're here today to talk to you about a $100,000 leadership commitment which would have a profound impact on the institution whose mission you believe in so fervently. Let me explain what your commitment will accomplish. . .

  There is no question that a statement like that will gain the attention of your prospect. The fund raisers who prefer to put the amount up front contend that it precludes the distraction of your prospect wondering how much you're going to ask for. After all, your prospect surely knows why you have come. It is contended that if you do not put forth the amount early the prospect spends her time wondering about the price tag. That may be true, but I prefer the ask at a later point in the call. With some of my donors, ones whom I know particularly well, I have indicated the expected level of giving early on, but these are the exceptions. My rejoinder to the fund raisers who contend that a figure should be put forth early is that if it is truly a stretch gift the prospect might lose concentration because of consternation. At any rate, I prefer to surface the figure at a later point. To gain attention, simply think out your first two or three statements and ensure that they are compelling. I do not believe in scripted solicitations because you become too focused on what to say next and I think they are somewhat demeaning to all involved. However, it never hurts to think about two or three opening sentences or phrases. During the call they can flow naturally and in your own style. An example of gaining attention might be:

> We're here today to talk to you about a once in a lifetime opportunity to enhance and extend the vital mission of an organization to which you have meant so much. We have an opportunity to profoundly impact the lives of future generations, and you are a special friend to whom we turn for the type of leadership necessary to achieve an important dream.

You get the idea.

- It is also important during the opening to gain common ground with your prospect. All things being equal, which is not always the case, you can gain common ground by recounting briefly the history of the donor's relationship with your organization. Even if it is somewhat tenuous, perhaps the only history being graduation from or treatment at your institution, a couple of statements about the prospect's connection to the organization will gain common ground. Of course, things will not be equal if the school has just called with the news that your prospect's son was expelled from school or the doctor phoned with bad news. We all understand that. However, taking a few minutes to reconnect the prospect to the organization in a personal way is what you want to accomplish. You can even combine this with gaining attention. Perhaps a comprehensive example of joining attention getting with common ground seeking will illustrate the point. Consider the following:

> Denise, you've been one of those caring and generous friends to whom we have always turned for support. You have served on our board for eight years and you have

been instrumental in our growth. You have generously contributed to the annual fund for as many years as I can remember, and your leadership and support was instrumental in the success of our first campaign. You and your family have had a long and special relationship with our organization. We are here today to discuss with you an opportunity to ensure excellence. We have a chance to make a huge difference in the lives of future generations who live and work in this community, and we would surely be remiss if we did not bring to you, our special friend, information about the possibilities which lie before us.

Now that you have gained common ground with your prospect and have her attention, you can move on to the next stage of the solicitation.

The opening should only consume about 10 percent of the allotted time.

III. PRESENTATION

- This phase of the solicitation should carry a relative weight, in terms of time expended, of 40 percent when compared to other elements. This is what we normally think of when we are asked about a solicitation. It is here that you present the project or opportunity. It is also at this point that you could lose the prospect. Out of necessity, presenting the case for support and the particular dynamics of a given project means that you do most of the talking. The danger is that your prospect's eyes may begin to glaze over and roll back into her head because she is not involved. You can lose the positive outcome if you are not careful. Here are some things we recommend to help you avoid that possibility.

- Talk about benefits and not features. This is basic marketing which we have discussed before. The benefits should be described in terms of human outcomes because this is what excites our donors the most. In his marvelous book, *Marketing Imagination*, Theodore Levitt asks whether Kodak markets the superior luminescence of its paper, or if it markets such things as remembrance and nostalgia. I once had a donor say to me,

> Bill, I've put up lots of buildings in my life. I don't need to hear any more about the number of rooms or the square footage involved. Tell me about the people who will pass through and work in this building. What will be accomplished because of its creation?

I couldn't explain my admonition any better than my donor.

- Now that we all agree to emphasize benefits versus features, let's further agree to keep our list short. The human tendency is to list all 20 benefits of a given opportunity because we are not sure exactly which ones will most interest our prospect. By the time we reach benefit number six, the prospect is confused and frustrated. Select what you believe to be the three or four most compelling outcomes and stress those. Obviously, if the prospect indicates an interest in other outcomes, by all means put those on your list. Just keep the list short.

- Another way to maintain interest is to ask questions. These do not need to be profound questions. They don't even need to follow the typology I will later present under active listening. You could even ask a question you know the answer to simply to get the prospect involved. You simply want the prospect acknowledging information or nodding his or her head so that there is some participation. Some examples:

"I am not always clear in my explanations. Did I explain that adequately?" "How do you feel about that?" "I need to know what you are thinking, Gary. What do you think about what we have discussed so far?" The point is to find a way to involve the prospect by asking questions.

IV. NEGOTIATION

This is where I prefer to mention the expected gift. It is well to remind ourselves to be clear, concise and precise in conveying the sought for commitment. We are seeking a specific amount for a specific outcome, and after mentioning the gift you should pause for a reasonable period of time. Unlike some theories of selling, I don't recommend a specific period for the pause, but it should be for longer than your visceral feelings tell you it should be. A pause of a few seconds can seem like eternity, but you want to be sure to give your prospect time to assimilate and react. It is a natural tendency to reinsert key points or benefits rather than permit a pause, but don't succumb to that. The pause is recommended because you need to know where your prospect stands. You also need to provide an opportunity for consideration and reaction. It is not because of the old aphorism, "The first one to speak loses." I become distressed when I hear that observation made. Fund raising is not a "win-lose" proposition. When done properly, it is "win-win," and we must sincerely believe that. It is too cute and contrived to say that the first one to speaks loses. It is just that you need to pause after making the ask in order to secure a reaction.

- It is at this stage in the solicitation that you will handle objections. More about those in a minute. In your outline, you should note those you expect, the recommended response and who should answer.
- This segment of the solicitation should have a time weighting of approximately 40 percent. Once again, you can place the initials of the person to make the

ask next to suggestions concerning phrasing and your
indication of the amount, opportunity and recognition. Of course, we all know that you never say, "We
have you down for . . . ." I find any of the following
to be quite acceptable:

> "Your commitment of . . ."
> "Your contribution/gift of . . ."
> "We seek your consideration of a gift of . . ."
> "We are seeking your leadership and ask-
> ing your consideration of a gift of _____
> to further our shared vision."

IV. CLOSING

- This segment is critical, although it will only receive
  about 10 percent of the time weighting. I recommend
  that you start this phase with what I call creative redundancy. By that I mean that you should again
  mention the opportunity presented, the two or three
  key benefits associated with the opportunity, and the
  expected commitment. Once again, you should pause
  following a recitation of the expected gift in order to
  allow your prospect an opportunity to react. It is also
  important that you limit your recitation of benefits
  to only two or three. You can reconfigure the benefits earlier mentioned, but it is fine to repeat what
  you have said before. Just keep the list short so that
  you do not confuse your prospect. I recommend
  creative redundancy for two basic reasons. First,
  repeating the benefits and expected gift represents
  a trial close. As we will soon see, you do not really
  expect the prospect to say "yes" at the initial major
  gift solicitation meeting, although that may happen.
  By mentioning again the central points and expectations, and pausing at that point, you provide the
  prospect with an opportunity to indicate an affirmative decision. Most major gift fund raisers think that
  if they secure an immediate "yes" they have not asked
  for enough. While that may be true, my recommen-

dation is that you thank the prospect profusely and declare a victory once you leave the premises. You will usually have another opportunity to seek an up-graded contribution, and probably much sooner than anticipated. You shouldn't worry about "leaving money on the table." After all, if you provide a satis-fying giving experience you will have another chance to present yourself. However, I have already men-tioned that you do not expect a commitment during the first solicitation call, which means that the trial close is not as compelling as the next reason for creative redundancy. The second and most impor-tant reason I recommend creative redundancy is that this conveys the preferred closing note for your meet-ing. You have covered much ground, discussed project particulars and handled objections. What you want to leave in the prospect's mind is an image of the benefits to be achieved, the opportunity to be funded (including recognition features) and the com-mitment necessary to achieve those results.

- Finally, in this phase you need to agree on the next step in the process. I recommend that you maintain control over the follow up, but not because of an attempt to manipulate. I have already observed that I do not feel intelligent enough to manipulate others, and to presume that this is possible is to place your-self in the win-lose mode. Maintaining control is simply a way to ensure timely follow-up and some degree of momentum. If urgency is lost a long term deferral or negative decision becomes increasingly likely. Also, if too much time passes your prospect is likely to lose clarity in his or her recollections of key benefits, outcomes and recognition opportunities. I recommend that you make a statement such as the following:

> I know you have much to think about and
> we deeply appreciate your consideration

of the opportunity to make a major difference in the important mission of the organization about which you care so much. I'll
give you a call Tuesday to respond to any
questions you may have and to discuss the
next step in the process.

But what if your prospect responds by saying,

I'll be out of town on Tuesday, but I'll be
sure to give you a call after thinking it over,?

How about,

I'll look forward to hearing from you. I
know that we are both on the run, and I'll
be sure to call if I do not hear by next Friday.

It is important to keep control in a caring,
professional way. One more thing about the follow-
up. I have learned that it is best undertaken by the
primary player. This is because the primary player
exerts the most influence, and therefore, will be the
most difficult person to avoid or put off. One of my
volunteers always used to tell prospects that he would
" . . . have Bill give you a call." I asked him to desist.
While I was aware of his busy schedule and I knew
that my request would entail a bit more expenditure
of time, I explained that it is much easier to put off
the major gifts fund raiser than it is a friend and
leader. He agreed. Our follow-up went much more
smoothly from that point forward.

When training fund raisers for solicitation I am careful to
emphasize that objections are something to be welcomed.
Objections are questions or statements reflecting an inadequate
understanding, a lack of information, concerns or obstacles to
the positive outcome. My esteemed colleague, Paul Edwards,
a key contributor to Stanford's first mega campaign and now

serving Promise Keepers, likes to say that "objections are your friend." While that sounds too cute, objections really are useful.

When I first started making solicitation calls, I wanted my prospect to avoid posing questions or making observations. Perhaps that's why we all need reminding to pause after we ask for a gift. I simply wanted the prospect to indicate an affirmative decision and allow me the chance to acknowledge and move on. There were, I am convinced, two basic fears at work. First, I was concerned that I might not have the information requested. Upon reflection I concluded that I will always have more knowledge about the institution or project than my prospects. If I happen not to have an answer to a particular inquiry, that is a positive because it gives me another pretext for follow-up. You don't look bad if you don't have at your fingertips every piece of information, and you have an opportunity to reconnect when this situation arises. I now say,

> That's an excellent question, and rather than hazard a guess, I'll check that out and give you a call on Tuesday. Thanks for bringing it up. I'm sure others will have the same question, and this will give me an opportunity to address an important issue.

You see, it's a positive, not a negative. But that is not really what really concerned me.

The second reason I hoped objections were not forthcoming was that I wished to avoid negativity. I was worried that there would be something substantive which would preclude the gift. I finally concluded, however, that if negativity existed, possibly standing in the way of a contribution, the condition existed whether I knew it or not. Better to know where you stand. If I am to have any opportunity at all to turn around a situation I need to know what the prospect is thinking. If you are successful at turning a negative into a positive the outcome can be quite exciting. I have observed that when you are able to ameliorate a concern the prospect returns to the fold as a roaring advocate. Some situations cannot be turned around, at least in the short term, but you need to know where you stand. Mark Twain once remarked of Wagner's music, "It's not as bad as it sounds." That holds true with objections as well. Generally the process of expiating is very beneficial to the prospect and makes it possible for you to move forward. Whether concerning a specific gift opportunity or broader relationship issues, the expression of concerns or gaps in understanding are a valuable tool for the alert fund raiser.

There are some excellent techniques for handling objections as they arise. These are not meant to be contrived or controlling. Rather, the idea is to facilitate communications or understanding. I do not recommend that you retain a list of these techniques in your briefcase for review just prior to a call. Rather, from time to time you can review the list and decide for yourself that you will use a given approach the next time a particular question or issue is raised. It really works, and you will be far more effective as a result. Here are some techniques for handling objections.

- *Question before responding.* For two reasons, it is often wise to question before answering an objection. First, it gives you an opportunity to formulate a response. Second, your questions may help to unearth a prospect's true concerns or motivation. Very often the prospect will create a "smoke screen" even though it is unintentional. He or she may not even know the true concern, but something just doesn't feel right or needs resolving. For example, when you ask for stretch gifts you expect some price resistance. If I know a prospect well I might respond to the expected objection, "That's a lot of money you're asking for," by saying something like,

  > We know it is and we do not take that lightly. However, you are one of the few people we can turn to for the sort of leadership necessary to accomplish this vital goal.

But I might also probe by asking, "Is it the timing or amount?" I once had a prospect respond by saying,

> I guess it's the amount. It just seems like a lot. And you know, I've never really understood what endowment means anyway. I guess that's where I let you invest the funds, although I'm sure you wouldn't achieve the results I'm used to, but endowment seems kind of abstract.

This prospect had stated that it seemed like too much money, but the real concern was lack of understanding and excitement about endowment gifts. The prospect was not even sure himself. It simply didn't feel right. In actual fact, it was too much for the gift opportunity just presented, although another approach could turn it around. It certainly would not have been too much for a project which garnered excitement. Probing before responding is very valuable.

- *Restate the objection prior to responding.* This is also an effective way to buy yourself a little time and elicit a reaction such that you gain a better understanding of the real concern.
- *If the objection is weak, you may choose to ignore it.* Be careful of this one. I only ignore objections when they fall into the category of "throw out lines." An observation that every time I visit it costs the prospect money might be ignored or laughed off. However, you should never ignore an objection if there might really be concern on the part of the prospect. An unanswered objection might block the gift, and real issues need to surface.
- *Never argue, only explain.* There may be times when you wish to argue with an irrational prospect who is casting aspersions at your institution or some of its leaders. However tempting that may be, never argue. You might win the argument, but you will surely lose the gift. The best thing is to listen attentively

while searching for meanings. One thing you can do is respond with relevant facts. You can say something like, "I understand completely your concern. I am sure others share that same concern. The only thing I can do is perhaps shed some light on the subject by revealing a couple of internal considerations which have not been made public. For example, . . ." You can cite some pertinent facts, and then move forward. But don't argue.

- *If an objection throws you off the track, return to the main issue.* Sometimes prospects will ask a question seemingly "out of the blue." If so, you must respond, but you should return to the central theme as soon as possible.

- *When an objection is true and real, you might admit it and move on.* If a particular concern or slightly negative observation is not central to the project or opportunity under discussion, you can acknowledge the premise and move on without much danger. For example, if I am seeking a gift for the oncology program at a hospital and a donor observes that the institution does not serve those suffering from burns, you can admit it without danger. You might say something like,

> It's true, we do not serve those who require that type of treatment. However, we are outstanding in oncology and have an opportunity to extend this excellence in service of others. That is exactly what we are talking about here today.

Your danger is that the objection concerns the program for which you are currently seeking funding. Then you need to use the next technique.

- *Convert a negative into a positive.* What if the prospect raises a negative objection concerning the specific program for which you are seeking support. You have no choice but to convert that negative into a positive. Actually, this technique for handling objections is helpful in many circumstances, most of which are less dramatic than the one under discussion, but this is a great way to prove the point. If, for example, the prospect expresses concern about the quality of the oncology program and that is the one for which you are seeking the gift, you must find a way to turn that around. Sometimes the gap is just too big and there is no credible way to accomplish this. However, you can often be successful with a little creativity. An example would be a response as follows:

> You are correct in stating that oncology has not received the attention it deserves. What is good about that is that our current leaders feel as you do. An oncology service of the highest possible quality is vital and the time has come to render it as outstanding as our other programs. Our leaders are committed to this, and it is visionary and caring friends such as you who will make this happen through vital private support.

I think you get the idea. At any rate, converting a negative into a positive is very effective.

- *A marvelous way to respond to an objection is to cite another donor who had a similar concern and explain how it was favorably resolved.* You should be as specific as possible. What I mean by that is that you might use the other individual's name, but only if you feel comfortable in doing so. If not, you can refer to the generic "friend" with a similar concern. Some examples may prove helpful. Let's suppose that your prospect expresses concern about the amount of the gift. You have probed and discovered that this is truly the case, and you have heard it more than once. You might respond as follows:

> Jerry had a similar concern. There is no question that we turn to leaders such as you and Jerry for vital support and we do not take that lightly. After reflecting on the major commitment and the importance of the program, Jerry decided that stretching the payments over a five to six year period would make it possible for him to support our shared objective. This may work for you as well.

One more illustration, this one concerning a more substantive objection, will make the point. I will assume with this one that we cannot use the other person's name because we do not feel comfortable in doing so without permission. The weightier the objection, the more important it becomes to be sure before using names. My example is a situation I actually confronted. The prospective donor launched into a diatribe about our organization's leadership because of a decision which dealt with an emotional issue tinged with political correctionness implications. I responded in the following manner.

> I understand completely what you are saying, and I am sure others share your concern. As a matter of fact, I recently visited with another close friend, one who is considering a major contribution to the campaign, and he was very vociferous in support of your position. Upon reflection, here's how he resolved the situation. He considered that organizational leaders come and go and that the process is somewhat cyclical. Sometimes we have effective leadership, and at other times we are not so fortunate. However, our friend knew that his support would live in perpetuity and outlast any particular administration.

He also reflected on the fact that his gift would support students and have nothing to do with our current leaders. He finally decided that the institution and the students were far more important than any particular administration and that the excellence of the program was more important than any one individual. It was the excitement about supporting students and ensuring excellence that led him to conclude that he should make the gift regardless of current personalities. I think he is now most satisfied that he decided to proceed.

You can see how citing another with a positive outcome allows you to urge someone to view the bigger picture without directly confronting their slight case of small mindedness. Citing another is most effective. Try it and I think you'll agree.

- *Where antagonism is present, hear out the prospect.* If necessary, drag out the problem through questioning. The tendency is to seek avoidance where antagonism is sensed. At least that's where I used to come from. I was hopeful the contentious issue wouldn't arise so that I could continue my discussion of marvelous opportunities. That approach is counterproductive. If antagonism is present and may block, either permanently or temporarily, a positive gift decision, it exists whether you know it or not. If the prospect is to feel better through venting or if you are to turn the situation around, you must know about the source of concern. I will make two or three attempts to have the prospect explain his or her concern in cases where I sense some antagonism, and I recommend that you do the same.

One of our most popular exercises at our seminars is the one concerning interpreting and responding to objections.

We utilize only real objections (I've heard them all), and I have noted after each a possible response and interpretation.

How to Learn from and Build on Objections

Consider the following objections and develop responses to three issues of importance: 1) What may be motivating the donor to react in this fashion? If there is a hidden agenda, what might it be? 2) How will you respond? Script an immediate response. 3) Might there be any long-term strategic implications attached to the objection? If so, how might your strategic approach be amended?

1. *That's a lot of money you're asking for ...*

   This is not generally a serious objection. You expect some degree of price resistance when you are seeking sacrificial gifts.

   Possible response: *We know it is, and we don't take that lightly. But you are one of the few people we can turn to for the necessary leadership to make this shared vision become reality.*

   Possible response #2: You might probe the prospect to see if the giving level truly underlies the objection. *Is it the amount or timing that concerns you most?*

2. *I'm not as wealthy as those folks who make those huge gifts you always read about.*

In this case, the prospect may be concerned about recognition or having an impact with his gift. This could be a case of the *small fish in a big pond* syndrome.

Possible response: *Every gift is important to us regardless of magnitude. Only with the help of many caring friends, joining together, can we achieve our important goal.*

Possible response #2: *There should be no mistake about the fact that what you are considering is most generous and will have a profound impact. It's not really a matter of the dollar level, rather the use of funds to impact human lives is what counts. In that respect, your gift is of particular significance.*

3.   *It's a great cause, but your timing is lousy. My business has "turned south" precipitously and I may even need to restructure some of my debt.*

Assuming this is more than a *smoke screen*, the objection is a serious one. At the very least, the prospect is not likely to be in a frame of mind to consider a major gift.

Possible response: *We are sorry to hear of your difficulties, but you are a proven winner and we know things will turn around for you. This is not a good time to discuss specifics about your gift opportunity, and we are grateful for the opportunity to make you generally aware of what we are seeking. Why don't we plan to reconvene at a better time and, in the meantime, please just know that we deeply appreciate your involvement. You are a special friend and we are grateful for all that you have done.*

Possible response #2: *We understand completely and recommend against making any immediate decisions. Perhaps what we should settle on is the opportunity just presented and what you would hope to do once your situation turns around. How do you feel about the general concept of the opportunity we just discussed?*

4. *It's a great cause, but your timing is lousy. My son just selected an expensive private college and my daughter is getting married in the fall.*

These are things which happen to all of us and while they may affect timing, they should not stand in the way of a gift decision. This is especially true if our understanding of the prospect's capabilities is accurate. Therefore, this may be a *smoke screen* for lack of passion, and the recommendation is to probe feelings about the opportunity presented. You can start by relaxing the prospect by way of positive and enthusiastic questions about the son and daughter.

5. *Your proposal about an Oriental wing for the museum is intriguing, and I'm sure the project (i.e., acquisitions funding) is important, but I'm really more interested in your collection of ancient civilization artifacts.*

Sometimes an objection like this indicates a lack of understanding relative to the opportunity. That is, the Oriental wing may indeed be compatible with an interest in ancient civilizations, and in this case education is needed. Otherwise, it is perfectly appropriate to ask questions about the prospect's interest in ancient civilization artifacts to see if some type of match can be made. The conundrum occurs if the museum does not have a collection pertaining to ancient civilizations. In this case, probing is recommended to see if a match is possible, although it may be that your museum will not become the organization of choice.

6. *I will need to see what my attorney and accountant have to say. I never do anything without their advice.*

   Recommended response: *Of course we want you to visit with your attorney and accountant. It is important to us that you receive good counsel and make your decision in the context of personal and family priorities relative to taxes and finances. All we really hoped to accomplish today was to reach agreement regarding this particular program and the support needed to make it become reality. The details are not unimportant and need to be addressed, but what I would like to know is your degree of shared enthusiasm for the opportunities we reviewed.*

7. *My accountant says I shouldn't give away any more money. Besides, I have all the deductions I can possibly use for the next few years.* (Instruction: Consider how your response would differ depending upon whether or not you perceive that the prospect is genuinely interested in your proposal.)

   Possible response: *It's important to us that you not do anything that doesn't make sense from a tax standpoint. Such details, while important, are not what we hope to resolve today. Rather, what we hope to ascertain is your shared enthusiasm for this opportunity and all that it will mean for others. How do you feel about the project and what will be required to achieve our objectives?*

Note: With numbers 6 and 7 you could indicate a willingness to visit with the advisors. This will only work a small percentage of the time, and it works best for major gifts fund raisers with a planned gifts background. If the meeting is not agreed to, you can then offer to write the advisor and inform him or her of earlier discussions. This gives you an opportunity to prepare the advisor in such a way that he or she is not insecure and does not resist because of lack of information. You can also say some very positive things about the prospect in the letter, and you want to be sure to copy the prospect and follow-up by telephone with all parties.

With number 7, you many have to go to the gift spread or a deferred arrangement. If the passion for the project exists, the giving method can be an answer.

8. *I'll need to think this over for awhile. It's a big decision. Why don't you give me some time and I'll get back to you?*

This seems to indicate a lack of passion, and you should do some probing about their understanding of and passion toward the opportunity. You should then take control of the follow-up.

Possible response: *Of course we understand your need to consider all we've discussed. In fact, we really want you to take your time to think about everything. What's your initial reaction to the opportunity and the benefits your gift would provide?* **Or,** *How do you feel about what we have discussed here today?* **Or,** *What questions do you have and what would be the key things you need to consider?*

9. *I'll do something, but I really can't do what you're asking for ...*

    (**Query:** Will your response differ depending upon your degree of confidence in the prospect's ability to give as requested?)

    If the prospect is capable of doing what you're asking for, this could be a case of inadequate cultivation such that you have not moved high enough on the priority list. It is possible to ask for too much, too soon, and this may be an example of what results, especially when you are dealing with an accumulator. It also could be a lack of passion about the outcome. Therefore, you could first probe the degree of enthusiasm for the particular project presented. At that point, after selling the dream, you should avoid *price haggling* because it conveys the wrong message and you can always come back another day.

    Possible response: *We deeply appreciate your support and your consideration of this once-in- a-lifetime opportunity. Whatever you decide will be the right outcome, but we would have felt remiss if we failed to present to you this exciting opportunity to make a huge difference in the lives of others. It is a lot to consider, and I'll plan to give you a call next Thursday to answer any questions you may have and to discuss the next step in the process. Don't forget, if the prospect promises to call you:*

    I'll look forward to hearing from you, and I know how busy we both are, so if I fail to connect with you by next Friday, I'll be sure to give you a call.

10. *Your presentation was interesting, but there are many fine causes competing for my attention.*

*There is only so much to go around and I'm al-
ready committed to several charities.*

This indicates a lack of passion and that your organization may not be high on the priority list. You need
to instill some passion, and the starting point would
be to probe the excitement over the outcomes associated with the opportunity presented. You might also
decide to suggest that this is merely a starting point
and that there is no hurry for a decision. This could
give you an opportunity for further involvement and
cultivation with outcomes (i.e., a visit to your facility).

11. *What are you coming to see me about?* (Calling for
the appointment.)

Possible response: *I want to discuss with you a
once-in-a-lifetime opportunity that I'm sure you will
find intriguing and exciting.* **Or,** *I would like to
discuss with you our campaign for excellence.*

You should not reveal any more than you need to,
and you hope that a one sentence response will suffice. If the prospect asks you to provide more detail
over the telephone, or to tell him or her how much
you're going to ask for, you should respond as follows: *I wouldn't do justice to you or the opportunity by reviewing the details over the phone. It
will only take about 20 minutes of your time, and
if Thursday would be better than Tuesday in that
regard I would be happy to adjust my schedule.*

If the prospect asks if you are going to request a
contribution you could respond as follows: *I do want
to talk with you about your leadership role in this
important effort.* **Or,** *I do not intend to ask you
for a gift. At some point I do want to talk to you
about your leadership role, but the purpose of this*

visit is merely one of informing you of what we believe to be a profound opportunity and securing your reaction.

The last response is one you can use when the relationship with the prospect is not solid. In those cases, it is often better to take it in two steps. Frequently, the prospect will ask you about the gift opportunity after you complete your presentation, but you can often secure the appointment when you make the prospect feel secure in this regard.

12. *I know that on paper it looks like I have a lot of money, but I'm too busy just trying to build my business to consider giving much away. I remember when I didn't have anything, and I also remember seeing people lose everything during the depression. I need to be careful, even about good projects.*

This is a difficult objection because it is obvious that you are dealing with an accumulator. What is perceived is real, and this type of insecurity often exists even with the extremely wealthy. If the project is amenable to a deferred gift (i.e., endowment) that may be the only method of giving which accommodates this psychology. Otherwise, you may have to lower your sights for now, or start the prospect on a long-term installment program.

Possible response: *I understand completely your need to continue to focus on your business. I also concur that you need to be very cautious because the economy cycles and personal and family priorities must always come first. What I have found with others is that if the opportunity is appealing there are often a number of ways to structure a commitment over a long-term. This allows you to* *retain flexibility in the use of your assets as needed, while ensuring in the long-run something you care about is accomplished. Some such gift arrangements are revocable so that you can even reverse field if necessary. All I really hoped to accomplish today was to acquaint you with a marvelous opportunity to make a difference, which I felt strongly would appeal to you based on my understanding of your interest. I would not want you to do it if it doesn't work or is contrary to your interests, and we could always explore details such as long-term or revocable commitments. How did you feel about the program and its impact on the beneficiaries of our service?*

13. *I'll need to talk it over with my spouse.*

   (**Instruction:** Consider how your response would differ, if at all, assuming 1) you know the spouse *is* important to the decision; 2) you're not sure if the spouse is important to the decision; 3) you don't know anything about the spouse; and 4) you know the spouse *is not* important to the decision.)

   Suggested response: *We are eager to have you talk it over with _____.*
   We were sure you would want to do this and perhaps it would make sense for all of us to get together early next week.

   Spouses discuss their philanthropy, so this is not a surprise. If the spouse is unimportant to the decision and you are sure of that information, this could be a put-off. However, the spouse should always be included in the proposal unless you are told otherwise by a natural partner. If the spouse has not been involved, you should always build in the offer to visit with him or her.

Suggested response #2: *Of course, we fully expected that you would want to talk it over with
_____ and we are eager to have you do so. We
would also be delighted to sit down with the two
of you next week, if this would prove helpful. For
now, we merely wanted to discuss the general possibilities and determine if you share our enthusiasm for the potential outcomes. How did you feel
about the project we discussed and its potential
benefits?*

14. *It's almost embarrassing for me to say this, but
    you're asking me for $1 million, and I really feel
    $100,000 is all I can spare right now.*

    Resist the temptation to negotiate price. This would
    make you look unprofessional, and sometimes the
    prospect makes an amazing transformation given a
    little time to consider everything. You can always come
    back at another time with other options at different
    giving levels. You may be forced, in some cases, to
    deal with other options, but it should be resisted. It is
    suggested that you let the prospect consider the op-
    portunity, and you can then assess where you are
    during the follow-up discussion. This may also be a
    case of inadequate cultivation, but if we assume that
    this is not true the response below would be merited.

    Suggested response: *Please do not in any way
    be embarrassed because there is nothing for you
    to be embarrassed about. Whatever you decide will
    be meaningful and deeply appreciated. However,
    because of the nature of the project and the de-
    gree to which we hold you in high esteem and con-
    sider you to be important to our organization, we
    would have felt remiss had we not illustrated for
    you this profound opportunity. That was really*

our only objective here today and why don't we give you some more time to consider everything. I want to again indicate that we deeply appreciate your consideration and all you have done for our shared enterprise. Whatever you decide upon will be greatly appreciated, I can assure you, and we look forward to our upcoming discussions.

And Just to Make Your Life a Little Easier...

15. *Would it be all right if I paid this over five years instead of the three years you mentioned?*

(**Instruction:** Don't spend too much time on this one!)

At our seminars I am often asked about closing techniques. I always preface my response with the observation that we are not capable of nor do we seek artificial control. The positive gift decision is the natural outcome of the entire moves management process which secures involvement and affirmation along the way. It is a culmination of careful planning and implementation. The techniques I prefer are simply designed to ensure clear communications and to adapt in a caring way to what we know about the psychology of decision-making. Those techniques designed to paint a prospect into a corner assume a "win-lose" equation, and I have already explained my distaste for that philosophy.

One thing I have observed about closing the gift is that it is important to read the signals and reach closure when the donor is ready. Over selling is tempting, but it can be harmful. If the donor has reached a positive decision, there is no reason to discuss details or benefits left unexplored. It is time to acknowledge and agree on the closing procedures. I have succumbed to the temptation to oversell and observed where it can be harmful. I recall a situation in which we were stopped at the door by a prospect who sought an explanation for an additional point which was intended as reinforcement. This particular matter became an issue before it was later resolved, and I tried to learn from that case of talking too much.

A few timely tips concerning the successful solicitation:

1. As you move toward closure, make sure that you maintain a positive attitude for the reasons earlier explored.
2. Maintain control of the follow-up process. This was another issue earlier addressed.
3. Make sure you give the prospect an opportunity to donate. Once again, this points to the use of an appropriate pause after asking for the gift.
4. Keep some selling points in reserve. I use this extensively in my gift solicitation activity. I have in the back of my mind two or three additional compelling benefits to mention in the event I need a little extra "push." Another approach is to have in mind another person for the prospect to meet with in reaching a decision. Primary players, or those with a great deal of influence over the prospect, are the best people to play this role. Sometimes I even leave a primary player out of a call simply to have another trump card to play. If you sense you need something additional or are lacking strong commitment, you are then in a position to say something like,

> We understand that these are not easy decisions. We are asking you to make a significant leadership commitment and we don't take that lightly. What may assist you in your deliberations is to spend a little time with _____ (e.g., primary player, curator, key researcher, etc.) as I think she might have some useful information to share. I know that she is most interested in this project and your personal role in making it become a reality. I will gladly arrange for the two of you to have some time together.

Holding something in reserve can be a most valuable tactic.

And now to some of the closing techniques I have found useful. The first is to use creative redundancy as explained in conjunction with the scripting format earlier provided. With this approach you mention again the most compelling outcomes or benefits associated with the project, the naming opportunity and the sought for commitment. You then pause in order to secure a response.

Another technique which has merit is to build a series of acceptances. In other words, you summarize the selling points, securing positive reactions along the way. It is usually best to proceed from the general to the specific. What I mean by this is that I start with a description of elements of the institutional mission with which I know the prospect agrees. I also make mention of earlier gift commitments made by the prospect and secure agreement as to the benefits and satisfactions which were gained. I then focus on the particular project, getting agreement as to the outcomes in human terms and the benefits to be realized. Finally, after presumably securing an affirmative nod of the head on each of the prior points, I indicate that the donor's commitment of the expected amount will help make that vision become a reality. As you build your series of acceptances, be careful not to be too repetitive in your questioning style. You can help yourself in that regard by occasionally making declarative statements or providing sidebar observations. You just do not want to appear too contrived in how you carry the prospect through the decision making process. One way to look at a series of acceptances is for you to review why you think the prospect should agree to a gift, being careful to assume the prospect's viewpoint. That is, what is the underlying logic, justification and excitement concerning the project, viewing it from the perspective of the donor's historical relationship with the organization. It is a recitation of why this particular opportunity is so compelling, starting with an overarching agreement and narrowing to the role the gift will play in achieving the shared objective.

The closing technique I like the most is often called the assumptive close. In other words, you assume that the gift is closed unless and until you are told otherwise. I do this naturally with every prospect. I begin talking in terms of "your endowment fund" or "your wing." It is a gentle, nonthreatening way to psychologically carry the prospect into a consideration of outcomes. It is also a great way to combine the outcomes with the attractiveness of recognition. It is neatly combined with the use of gift agreements, which is something I will discuss later in the book. I've only been called on the assumptive close once, and even then it was nothing to be concerned about. I'm thinking of the time I was explaining to a donor the exciting outcomes to be funded by his endowment. I also observed that his endowment would stand as lasting testimony to his thoughtfulness and to his very special relationship with our institution. He then remarked, "I didn't say that I would make the gift." I responded, "Oh, I know that. I'm simply speaking in terms of possibilities. But what truly excites me about your fund. . ." As you can see, I returned to the assumption without trepidation!

What makes the job of the fund raiser challenging is the fact that the potential outcomes from a major gift solicitation are several, and all but one require judgment and interpretation. Let's consider the possible solicitation outcomes comparing a sustaining gift with a major gift. This can be illustrated as follows:

Call Outcome Possibilities

Small Gift	Major Gift
	Gift
Success: Gift	or
	Advance
Failure: No-Gift	Continuation
	or
	No-Gift

With the sustaining gift you receive a "yes" or "no" and move on. With a major gift, it's not so simple. You could secure an affirmative response, although most of us do not expect this outcome where the solicitation is for a stretch or sacrificial commitment. If we secure a positive response, we are convinced we did not ask for enough. As explained earlier, any time this happens you should declare a victory. But what you realistically hope for is an advance as opposed to a continuation. Let me give you an example of each.

An advance might consist of a reaction such as the following:

> That's a lot of money you're asking for. I've never really thought in those terms, although I must admit the project is exciting. It is also attractive to me to consider having my family's name permanently associated with the hospital. I just need to think about the amount and how it could possibly be done. You know that I love the institution and will do everything in my power to ensure the success of the campaign. You have my commitment to doing whatever I can, but I just need time to think about something this big.

That, in my mind, is an advance. A continuation might be more like the following:

> That's a lot of money you're asking for. I appreciate your thinking of me, but it's hard to consider that amount given all of my other interests. As you may know, I'm very involved with the museum and the church, and I have committed major sums to their campaigns. I've never really thought of the hospital on those same terms, and I want to warn you that I'm not likely to stretch to the level you're hoping for. I'll help out, but I hope I don't disappoint you when I say that I'm not likely to do anything near what you're asking.

That's more of a continuation. It certainly does not mean you won't secure a commitment, and, who knows, if you work hard enough you may eventually get what you are seeking.

However, it's obvious that you have a long way to go with this prospect.

The process is even more complicated than that. There are really four types of "no" and it's our job to determine which type we have received. One form of "no" is "no forever," or at least for the foreseeable future. A second possibility is "no to that amount but not to another amount." You might also hear, "no to that project but not to another project." And finally, the negative response might mean "no at this time, but perhaps I will do it at another, more propitious time."

You can see that the possibilities are many and will require your judgment. That's why active listening is so important and how the discussion of possibilities prove of value. After all, major gift fund raising is more of an art than a science. What you need to do is trust your instincts and judgment.

Some valuable research will help you interpret "no" and assist you in determining which of the four types a given response represents. Some years ago philanthropists were queried, not about gift opportunities they seized, but about those they declined. It is fascinating to examine things from the negative perspective because it often better highlights the key points to be made. The survey was not intended to be a probability sample, and the responses were categorized in ways which make sense from a fund raising viewpoint. There is not a rank ordering of responses, but to make the list there would have been a sufficient number who expressed the underlying sentiment. Keeping all of that in mind, here are reasons prospects said "no" to one or more gift solicitations:

- *A mismatch of interests.* This is where you seek a gift for the wrong project. It is not necessarily a long term gift "killer," but soliciting for the wrong project will certainly lead to at least a temporary "no." You might ask how such a mismatch of interests could occur if effective listening was taking place during the process of making cultivational moves. Certainly, there are those cases where this occurs due to false assumptions on the part of the fund raiser or a failure to probe and listen. However, even when you do everything right there will be those solicitations where the particular opportunity is not the perfect one for the given prospect. This is simply due to the nature of the process. When you ask people for sacrificial gifts they sometimes think in different terms. It may not matter at the sustaining gift level, but when you consider a major gift you are led to a determination of how you would like to make an impact in this world. You may never have thought of this before. I have seen cases where the major gift solicitation is the catalyst for the prospect considering the kind of legacy he or she would like to leave in life. I recall asking a staff member to handle a gift closing at a distant site. My schedule just wouldn't permit my traveling that far, and I told the prospect he would like this staff member better because he played golf. My colleague returned after closing the gift and preliminarily discussing with the prospect the ultimate use of the fund to be created in his name. I knew of the prospect's keen interest in an athletic program at our university, but my colleague asked if I was aware of an interest in theater. The prospect had asked that 50 percent of the endowment income be directed to the theater program. I was astounded and called a natural partner who knew the prospect well. I asked if he was familiar with the prospect's interest in the theater. At first, my natural partner expressed surprise, but then he reflected upon the prospect's undergraduate days many years prior. He said,

> Now that I think about it, he had a burning interest in becoming an actor. I don't think he was talented enough, and business necessities took him elsewhere. But maybe he's carried this dream with him all of these years.

I finally concluded that when considering how to make an impact the prospect wanted to help others pursue the dream he never could. This was a mismatch of interests easy to deal with, but it makes the point that it will happen when you ask people to consider actions with lasting effects.

- *A premature request.* What this really points to is inadequate cultivation or involvement. Sometimes we are forced to a premature solicitation due to the existence of a campaign or because of our own impatience. I think if given an opportunity many prospects would explain a premature request by saying,

> I think of your organization at the $1,000 level. I think of my church and the museum at a much higher level, but I have been far more involved with those institutions than with yours.

We must remember that donors give for their reasons and not ours. No matter how compelling the need or the campaign in our minds, we must involve the donor in the vision if we are to maximize our opportunity for success with stretch solicitations.

- *A failure to ask for a specific gift or action.* We should always strive to structure our requests as clearly as possible. This explains why we recommend solicitations for specific amounts and purposes. If you wonder how there could be a solicitation with a failure to ask for a specific gift, just ask the experienced professional if he or she has had a volunteer "choke" on the ask. I have. Some volunteers I am acquainted with enjoy making solicitation calls, but they just can't bring themselves to be specific when it comes time to seek the commitment. When prospects are confused, they will demure. Sometimes confusion even obscures recollection. I had a colleague remark that he was astounded when a prospect on the way out of a restaurant asked, "Did you just ask me for a gift of $1

million?" My friend was very assertive in his solicitations and was always very clear as to amount and
purpose. He swore that this was the case this time. I
asked him how much time had elapsed between the
gift request and the end of the meeting. He recalled
that well over an hour had transpired. During that
time they had finished their wine and talked about
many other issues. I observed that it was clearly a
case of selective hearing and some degree of confusion. That's another reason for the creative redundancy I recommended earlier. The expected action
must be made clear.

- *A failure to ask for enough.* This sometimes astounds
  people, but I have observed situations where this has
  occurred. I think there are two cases where a failure
  to ask for enough leads a prospect to decline. One
  case pertains to what is known in the jewelry business as prestige pricing. Savvy jewelers know that at
  a certain range on the demand curve, if you raise the
  price of a given item the quantity sold actually increases. There is a perceived value/price relationship. I have found this to be true from time to time in
  fund raising. For example, at my institution we used
  to woefully under price endowed chairs. I believe the
  idea was to bring the threshold down to the stretch
  level of major donors who could not otherwise fund
  a chair. The problem was, we were tarnishing the
  image of an endowed chair. We had donors wonder
  why a chair at the University of Chicago or Harvard
  was so much more expensive. The questions raised
  seemed to be along the following lines:

> What is wrong with our endowed chairs?
> Are our chairs not as prestigious? Do we
> use our chairs to hire average as opposed
> to excellent faculty members?

We should have made other opportunities attractive
to our prospects rather than underachieving with

chairs. Thresholds which reflect the importance and prestige of the opportunity must be maintained.

- *An excessive request.* When I first got into the business I was told that you could not ask for too much. To ask for something beyond capability was to flatter a prospect. I have found, simply, that this advice was wrong headed. You can ask for too much and look stupid in the process. I remember an incident during a campaign where a woman was to be asked for approximately 100 percent of her net worth. It didn't take a seminar or book to tell me that the target was ridiculous. But that is not what I'm talking about when I address the issue of asking for too much. Even if a prospect is capable, you can go too far and too fast. If someone's largest single gift to any charitable organization is $50,000 and you are considering a $1 million proposal, you might wish to pause for reflection. Even if the prospect has made a $1 million gift to another charitable organization, if the largest single commitment to your cause has been $5,000 you might want to plan some intermediate giving levels before going to seven figures. The point is to avoid going too far, too fast. You don't look too professional when that happens. I remember years ago being involved in one such embarrassing situation. I recall during our strategy meeting raising a concern about an eight figure solicitation when the largest single commitment to our organization was at five figures. It just didn't seem right to me, but I was younger then and deferred to a veteran. The solicitation call became embarrassing when we realized we had gotten ahead of ourselves and the prospect began apologizing for his inability to meet our expectations. In fact, he almost apologized for the $1 million he was prepared to contribute. It was not a pretty situation, and I learned a great deal from it. You can certainly ask for too much.

- *A failure to convey urgency.* We must render our projects important and urgent to our prospects. Good presentation style and an emphasis on outcomes is of value here. It is not too difficult to convey urgency about bricks and mortar because a building project requires near term funding. But what about endowment? Why not try to give the decision urgency with the following type of message: "Your commitment now, regardless of the timetable by which it is fulfilled, will ensure our success and serve as an inspiration to others."

- *Appearance of difficulty.* It is important to make giving as easy as possible, which means that appropriately timed spreading and gift methodology options may prove of value. Be careful, however, because too much emphasis on technique can confuse a prospect and cause him or her to demure.

- *A mismatch between the solicitor and prospect.* We talked before about finding a solicitor who displays knowledge, commitment and passion. I remember one session between a prospect and a primary player, the latter having all of the perfect attributes. The prospect and the volunteer were peers in every sense, had known each other for years, and had an almost identical net worth. It was perfect on paper, but something seemed wrong in the meeting room. Upon later reflection with a colleague who attended the meeting, it was concluded that there was a spark of rivalry to be the biggest fish in our somewhat modest pond. We never again used that primary player with that particular prospect. It doesn't always defeat the gift on a permanent basis, but a mismatch between a solicitor and a prospect can extend the process.

- *A failure to include the spouse was among the reasons prospects said "no."* It is important to include the spouse, and it becomes increasingly so as the magnitude of the sought for gift increases. It may not be vital to involve a spouse at the sustaining gift levels, but it is likely to be critical where a stretch gift is sought. Spouses discuss their philanthropy, and guessing about interpersonal dynamics between spouses is speculative at best. At one of our seminars a philanthropist said,

> We always discuss our big gifts. He has causes of importance to him, and there are certain organizations with which I have greater involvement. We take the lead on different issues, but the point is that we discuss everything.

But what to do if you have never involved the spouse? The first thing I suggest is to go to a natural partner and inquire about the situation. On a couple of occasions I was told not to involve the spouse because of impending fissure in the relationship. But almost always I am told to somehow seek spousal involvement. How do you do that? One way is to be sure that the spouse's name is included on the proposal. Prospects may not always read proposals, but I like to put the name of the proposed fund or wing in boldface and that is usually noticed. Just make sure that the spouse's name also appears. In addition, during the solicitation you can offer to arrange for a follow up visit with the spouse. The prospect can then tell you that it is not necessary, but at least you have acknowledged an interest in including the spouse. It is important, so do everything in your power to include the other partner.

- *A failure to sell the dream.* Remember, people give because they want to have an impact in an area of importance and wish to achieve outcomes in human terms. We must present the gift opportunity in a compelling way from the prospect's viewpoint and convey how the gift will satisfy values which are personal to the prospect. The giving opportunity is a vehicle by which shared values between the prospect and the organization are achieved.

- *A failure to follow up was mentioned by many philanthropists as the reason for declining a gift opportunity.* The responsibility falls squarely on the shoulders of the development professional, and a failure to follow up is never excusable. Indeed, we know that urgency is important so follow up must be prompt and vigorous.

- *Poor timing was a reason for saying "no."* There is not really much you can do about timing except to be aware and sensitive. You hope that natural partners alert you to any major timing issues of which they are aware, but sometimes there is just no way to know in advance. As illustrated in our exercise on responding to objections, some timing issues are more serious than others. I once had a prospect inform me that due to some serious illegal activities on behalf of key personnel his company was about to be liquidated which would generate little net of debts and legal expenses. Now that fits the definition of poor timing! There was little to be done except to come back another day when, presumably, things would be more sanguine.

Understanding why prospects might say "no" is of obvious importance. After all, it could always be a negative of the non-permanent variety. The art involved is that of interpreting what the response really means. An intriguing article in *Fundraising Management* some years ago, written by B. Worth George from Pilgrim Place, discussed the possible interpretations of a declination. I think George's material must have drawn from some of Cialdini's research at Arizona State. George enumerates several possibilities which may underlie a temporary declination. Among them:

- *A transitional response because of confusion.* If a prospect is confused he or she will demur or say "no." It may not be permanent, but when any of us are confused we often postpone a decision. That is why we recommend a solicitation which is concise, precise and specific. It also helps explain why I attempt to avoid a list of alternative opportunities and a discussion of more than one giving level. When you are confused, you quite naturally postpone your actions. I recall shopping for a replacement computer and being assisted by a young man who was obviously well schooled in the subject. The problem was that he confused me with baud rates and other esoteric terms. I delayed the decision until I could check with a neighbor who was more knowledgeable and experienced in this vein. I later bought the computer, which illustrates that confusion does not always permanently destroy the outcome. However, there was a delay which could have been avoided had the young man simply told me that the computer had the desired features and would serve well my objectives. Confusion is an enemy to the desired outcome.

- *A "It doesn't feel right . . ." response.* We have all witnessed this response from time to time. The problem is, it is very difficult to determine the reason why the prospect doesn't "feel right." It could be because of extraneous influences. It could also be because we're asking for the wrong amount or purpose. The only way to attack this reaction is to seek to unearth the prospect's concerns through active listening. In other words, you need to probe through questions to determine the underlying reason for a less than enthusiastic response. I have been known to say, "I sense some concern or hesitancy on your part. I would like to know what you are thinking." If "it doesn't feel right" then the process is surely delayed and I need to know the reason for this if I am to get the solicitation back on track. Until then, as long as the prospect is feeling out of sorts you will receive a "no" of one of the types earlier described.

- *A prospect defers or demurs where passion is lacking.* We have already discussed this possibility, but isn't it interesting that another source is reinforcing the need for selling the "dream"?

- *A lack of understanding may be a reason for receiving a "no."* Again, the need to be specific and precise is reinforced.

- *A prospect, if he or she does not see why the commitment is crucial at the current time, may demur.* This is reinforcement for the earlier statement that it is important to demonstrate urgency to a prospect if you are to receive affirmative action.

- *A "no" of one of the four types will occur if the prospect fails to see his or her expected benefit from the gift transaction.* I have left solicitations and lamented that we were sidetracked and failed to emphasize strongly enough the recognition or benefits which would most motivate that particular donor. With one particular donor we only mentioned in passing the permanent naming of a wing, and I later commented that we were remiss because there was little question this would be the most compelling motivational trigger. On another occasion we were visiting with a prospect who clearly sought prestigious association with our highest level board members and our president. Yet we somehow never mentioned our desire to have our president and board members meet with him and how pleased they would be with his involvement. It is easy to get sidetracked during solicitations, but we should never fail to visit the recognition or other dynamics which are critical to our prospects. If someone fails to see that they will receive the psychic values of importance, a decision is easily delayed in favor of a search for a more satisfying relationship.

- *A "no" might mean that the prospect did not relate well to the solicitor.* This was explored elsewhere, but the fact that it was again mentioned reinforces its importance.
- *A prospect will decline an opportunity, perhaps only temporarily, because of a lack of philanthropic experience.* The longer I go the more I realize the salutary effects of philanthropic experience. I used to express chagrin when I heard of one of my prospects donating to another cause. As mentioned, I don't sell against other charitable opportunities; indeed, I help my donors assist worthy organizations. However, I am like any other fund raiser in that when I'm intensely seeking a commitment I worry when another giving alternative appears to be of higher priority. Well, I needn't have worried. My response should have been to comment about how wonderful it was for the prospect to support that given cause. If the giving experience was favorable there it would make it easier when I solicited a much more significant gift. As we earlier reviewed, the simple fact is that giving begets giving when it is all done properly.

Aryeh Nesher likes to talk about those things which can impede a solicitation. I have added to his list of impediments, just as you can add to mine. Impediments to an effective solicitation include the following:

1. *Inadequate preparation.*
2. *Insecurity.* This is related to preparation in that rehearsing and preparing, not to mention experience, help to build confidence.
3. *Assuming too much about your prospect and his or her potential interest in the project at hand.* Nesher describes this as self-deception, and what he refers to is our tendency to assume that genealogy and interest will translate into a major gift commit-

ment. We must always view the situation from our potential donor's perspective, not from ours.

4. *Failure to listen prior to asking.* Remember to follow Jerry Panas' dictum, "listen the gift." A failure to probe through active listening means a greater potential for assumption and self-deception.

5. *Premature selling of the "product."* This is selling from the fund raiser's perspective, not from the donor's. Once again, assessing interest and the potential for shared values with the mission of your organization is crucial. Too often we begin selling the project, or the giving method in the case of the deferred gift specialist, before we even probe and assess a prospect's interest. We are admonished to listen and learn.

6. *Emphasis on features as opposed to benefits and outcomes is an impediment to an effective solicitation.*

7. *Embracing the "win-lose" style as opposed to the "win-win" style is a certain impediment to your success.*

I hope that all of these tools and techniques help you in gaining the confidence to undertake solicitations with enthusiasm. When a prospect says "no" it is not personal to you, nor does it reflect on the importance of the mission of the institution. In fact, as we have learned, it may be a "no" on way to a "yes."

It is important to acknowledge that there is no one solicitation approach that will ensure success. I am concerned when fund raisers ask me for my terminology because another style of presentation can be equally effective. If in the course of our conversations with prospects we slip and emphasize features or say the wrong thing, it should not be of concern. This is a long term process affected by many variables and psychological building blocks. To attribute a "no" to one particular sentence or incident is to fail to recognize the complexity and enormity of the nurturing fund-raising dynamic.

Perhaps you will be emboldened by my story of a solicitation disaster. There is an object lesson to my telling this story,
which I will share with you shortly. The incident I am thinking
of occurred during a major campaign effort. I was asked by
one of our staff members to take his place on a solicitation
call because of his need to leave town for a family emergency.
The request was for a $100,000 gift to help meet a challenge
grant for an endowment in furtherance of the fine arts program. The income would be utilized to attract outstanding
classical performers and allow them some time with professors and students. It was a worthy program.

I asked my colleague if the volunteer solicitor had read
the proposal and if adequate training had taken place. I was
assured that this had been accomplished. I was a bit surprised
that this volunteer solicitor was being employed because I had
known him for some years and was unaware of his interest in
the fine arts. In fact, I was a little surprised that he had not
contacted me prior to making a gift commitment as we usually discussed his giving plans. Nevertheless, I went blithely on
my way anticipating no particular difficulties.

I picked up my volunteer solicitor at his office, and we
only had a few minutes until we reached the office of our
prospect. I asked if he felt adequately prepared and if he had
reviewed the proposal. He stated that he felt fine about everything but would prefer that I make the actual solicitation. This
was not particularly unusual, so I thought nothing of it at the
time. I recall the solicitation taking place on a Friday after-
noon, and I was feeling great about the impending weekend.
The weather was nice, and it seemed a great day to ask for a
gift. I felt good about the presentation because I was stressing
benefits and outcomes. I seem to recall painting a picture of
Pavarotti in the classroom, and I thought this so compelling
that I was tempted myself to help meet the match. My problem was that I was too trusting and had not done any probing
of the prospect. I would have been better off had I asked questions and followed my own dictums about active listening.

I reached the critical point of the solicitation and boldly
asked for the sought for contribution in order to accomplish a

shared dream. This was followed by an appropriate pause. My prospect responded by saying, "That's a lot of money you're asking for." This did not disturb me as I expect this sort of objection with a stretch request. I responded, "We know it is and we do not take that lightly. But you are one of the few people we can turn to for the sort of leadership necessary to accomplish this important vision." I paused again. It was now my volunteer's time to intervene, and he made the following statement: "It really is a lot of money. Denise and I aren't even sure that we can do it yet."

Now the pause was extremely pregnant with meaning, and I felt the perspiration beading on my neck. The little voice inside my head kept asking me what I should say, and I finally decided I would ignore my volunteer's observation. I then started to launch into a reiteration of the key benefits of a named endowment for the fine arts, but I was interrupted by our prospect. He said,

> But that's not the biggest problem, Bill. I really have no interest in the fine arts. I've only been to the fine arts center once, and that was when my wife dragged me there. I'm really a football guy. If I were to make a gift of that magnitude, and it is a lot of money, it certainly would not be to the fine arts.

What do you say to that? The beads of sweat had turned into a torrent and the back of my shirt was dripping wet. It was one of those moments where there is nothing you can say and maintain some pretense of intelligence. Whatever I was to say was sure to sound stupid, and that was certainly the case. I said something like "Well, this is helpful information."

How's that for dumb? I finally recovered and added something like,

> I think we owe you the kind of excitement and satisfaction the fine arts endowment provides those who are interested in that program. Our campaign is big and diverse, and I'm quite sure there are opportunities which will provide you with the pleasure you would expect from a major commit ᷉ nt. If you would allow me, I would

like to begin exploring your areas of interest and ways of having an impact that would be satisfying to you. May I ask you a few questions?

We went on from there.

What is interesting to consider is that this kind gentleman eventually did make a gift to our campaign. He donated $50,000 and had an impact in a way which reinforced his values in life. I have reflected upon that outcome, and the fact that I survived the incident without harm. Of course, I wanted to humiliate the colleague who was so ill-prepared, but it is interesting that this disaster still lead to a positive outcome.

One of the object lessons is that the case overrides all and that with integrity and effort you will succeed. You should take strength from the knowledge that there will never be a worse solicitation than the one just described, but somehow it still lead to a gift. There was nothing wrong with that warm, kind gentleman, nor was there anything wrong with me. Certainly, I would be sure to do better the next time, but I had done my best in representation of a mission of importance. Another object lesson is the fact that there is no one precise way to express our presentation that will ensure our success. The process is bigger, more complex, and subject to more telling variables than our mere verbal articulation of the case.

I want you to feel encouraged to enter into solicitations in a way which is natural to you, and you should have confidence that you will succeed because you have integrity and represent an institution of importance. I hope this little vignette also reinforces the need for adequate preparation.

A solicitation is simply another move in the process of relationship building. However, we must recognize that at certain points in the relationship it is vital to ask. Bernie Neufeld once said, "It's amazing what you don't get when you don't ask." He had a point.

It is even more important that we accept the premise that the process of asking is offering people an opportunity to express life values and to make a difference in this world in a way that is personally gratifying to them. And let us never forget that once the gift is secured, the process of cultivation really begins in earnest.

I agree with Theodore Levitt when he averred, "The era of the one night stand is gone. . . The sale (gift) merely consummates the courtship, at which time the marriage begins."

Finally, Henry Ford stated that "Obstacles are those frightful things you see when you take your eyes off your goal." Your goal is worthy, just and important. Therefore, you should proceed confidently to seek support from those whose values are reflected in the important missions of the organizations you represent.

9

Active Listening —
The Essential Tool for
the Successful Major
Gifts Fund Raiser

Listening is a learned skill. It's a good thing because it is absolutely essential to the effective major gifts fund raiser. An informal poll of colleagues concerning the traits most important to a major gifts fund raiser revealed something very interesting. There was general agreement about the top ten, but there was precise and unanimous agreement concerning the two most important traits. The first characteristic of importance, and one which cannot be learned, is impeccable integrity. You've got to have it. It can't be learned and there is no substitute. Of course, you can conduct a session in ethical decision making, but either you have integrity or you don't.

The second important characteristic for an outstanding fund raiser, fortunately one which can be learned, is effective listening. There just isn't a substitute. The goal of the effective listener is to encourage the prospect to talk, then listen in order to understand his or her views, unique needs and fears relating to the gift decision. To be effective requires that you listen without an agenda. It is in this manner that you can truly become a partner and consultant to your prospect as he or she works through the gift decision.

Sales Effectiveness Training contains some valuable insights concerning active listening. Zaiss and Gordon explain why we are often not effective at listening. They enumerate the following:

- **We've never learned how to listen.** How many courses have you attended where you are taught how to be an effective listener? I've attended communications lectures where I was exposed to the theory of sender and receiver, but I don't recall being taught active listening techniques.
- **We may not be effective at listening because of a belief that fund raising is talking.** This is a trap which is easily fallen into. We think of presenting, not listening, but it is the latter which will win us major gifts.
- **Effective listening requires focus and concentration.** Many of us have a difficult time with that.
- **Our paradigms distort what we hear.** We all understand the concept of selective perception or interpretation, and it's impossible to avoid. However, recognizing our own paradigms and how they might affect what we hear from others will help us become more effective at strategic relationship building.

Zaiss and Thomas break listening skills into three basic components. First is what they call attending behavior or nonverbal communications. Nonverbal communications can be very clear in demonstrating to the other person that you care about what he or she is saying. Interpreting and employing nonverbal communications are admittedly important, but I want to caution here against getting too carried away. In my opinion, some of the theories of nonverbal communication border on psycho babble and are of little practical use. Of course, I understand that if I enter an office and the prospect is in the fetal position he or she may be somewhat defensive. But I truly think the theories get carried away. Whether someone rests his chin in the left hand as opposed to the right has little

Freudian significance in my mind, and we run the risk of obfuscating communications when we over interpret.

The second type of listening is passive. Silence can be a powerful tool. You can utilize silence to demonstrate that you are paying attention to the speaker. It is also true that using pauses or silence helps you avoid snap judgments or make defensive responses. Silence helps you reason through your interpretations. Finally, passive listening is an effective tool because it creates mild pressure for the speaker to keep on talking.

Active listening is the form we normally think of, and most of our techniques fall into this category. This is because active listening is proactive. It involves the use of questions to elicit and clarify information. The use of questions forces you to concentrate on what the prospect is saying and helps you understand and empathize.

A great way to conceptualize the process of communications was provided by Sarah Arciszewski in an article published some years ago. She talked about the two basic modes of communication. The first mode is known as survival. This is typified by pauses, insecurity and a concern with yourself. It is a me/me form of conversation, and what we mean by that is that you are more concerned with what you are going to say next than with what the other person is communicating to you.

The second mode is known as connection. This is a natural flowing conversation between two people who feel comfortable with each other. This is a me/you form of conversation whereby you are truly open to receiving information from the other person. We always seek the connection mode, and the techniques I will enumerate later will assist you in achieving that state.

We all slide between survival and connection many times during the course of a day, even within the same conversation. Consider your own conversations and how you are sometimes halting, unsure and uncomfortable. With some people that's all there is. At other times, you may do certain things to help you to move to the natural, flowing state, and the tools provided later will prove helpful in that regard.

If you haven't read *Conceptual Selling* you may want to set aside some time for it. It has a great deal to share relative to relationship building and active listening. One of the observations is that basic issues sometimes stand in the way of receptivity to messages. I think this concept is particularly germane in major gifts fund raising where we are asking people for sacrificial commitments. Many insecurities and issues can enter into the decision making process. It may not be of concern at the lower levels of giving, but as we increase the size of the solicitation we need to be on the lookout for the insecurity associated with basic issues. We are talking here about how the prospect feels he or she may lose or be diminished by the release of assets, and as much as possible, it is important for us to probe a prospect's feelings and help resolve them. To a large extent, it may even be out of our control. Basic concerns which may stand in the way of the positive gift decision include the following:

- Loss of power
- Loss of control
- Failure to achieve self-recognition
- Loss of flexibility
- Loss of security

Obviously, the basic issues overlap. It also is apparent that these concerns often have deep psychological roots and there is little we can do to change how the prospect feels. I have found, however, that awareness of the issue on the part of the prospect helps him or her arrive at an accommodation. The basic issue of recognition is one we can control and emphasize with our prospects, but for the most part the rest are givens which we can only help our prospects resolve internally. Consider the prospect who is a product of the depression and the economic insecurity that went along with it. A fear about control, flexibility or security is bound to exist in one form or another.

Earlier in the book I pointed out how as staff members and volunteers we are important to prospective donors because we are the tangible substitutes for our organizations. If we instill confidence, we can help our prospects overcome fears and obstacles. We can render the case real to prospective donors and when they have confidence in us they will feel better about their charitable investment. Therefore, it is important for us to do our best to establish credibility.

Social scientists tell us that credibility can be earned, which is the strongest form but perhaps the most time consuming. Credibility can also be transferred to us through association. I utilize that concept by carefully selecting natural partners to go along with me on a call. Early in my planned giving career I had a difficult time in achieving credibility. I was just too young and many of my elderly prospects wanted to treat me like a son. Unfortunately, I long ago stopped having that problem, but it was very real at the time. The way I would overcome this was to ask an older colleague or volunteer to go along on a call and shamelessly espouse my experience and professional capabilities. I was seeking to have credibility transferred to me. Finally, you achieve credibility through reputation, which is the weakest form and can be lost without performance.

Experience helps you establish credibility with a prospect because some degree of knowledge is associated with it. Obviously, a powerful demonstration of knowledge is another way to earn credibility. Where this issue becomes important you should search for those contexts where you have the opportunity to demonstrate your knowledge. This can be especially important to the planned gift fund raiser. An effective presentation style or presence also helps you establish credibility.

Relevant to our discussion of active listening is what psychologists tell us about maintaining credibility. Once gained, credibility can be maintained with a prospect or donor in the following fashion:

• By asking relevant questions;

- By listening intently;
- By being yourself;
- By avoiding the temptation to be a "know it all";
- By demonstrating that you sincerely care;
- By producing the giving experience promised or by following-up promptly and professionally with the agreed upon next step; and
- By focusing on the prospect throughout the process.

Active listening entails asking questions. Once so acknowledged, the issue becomes the types of questions you need to formulate. I have researched many sources for a workable typology. *Spin Selling* has an excellent framework and is a book you should consider adding to your library. The best framework, in my opinion, is put forth by *Conceptual Selling*.

There are four basic types of questions you should be asking your prospects as you move through the cultivation process. In a very loose way I will list them in chronological order and from the least to the most complex. That is, the first two types are ones you are likely to ask with greater frequency early in the cultivation process. The last two are a bit more complex in structure and response. This is only a general trend, however, and should not be taken too literally. You will ask all of these types of questions throughout the process. The typology I recommend you consider is as follows:

- **Confirmation Questions.** These are questions designed to validate data or point out inaccuracies in your understanding. Before making a call, consider what you know about the prospect, or think you know, and formulate some questions to confirm this. Certainly, I often seek to confirm what research has told me about the individual. You will ask a lot of confirmation questions without even knowing how you might use the information. You are weaving a tapestry and no one strand is all that important. Occasionally, there will be a confirmation question of great import. For example, I had decided to ask a prospect to establish a scholarship fund in honor of her family with awards being issued to recognize each of five brothers and sisters. It was crucial that I confirm the number, status and relationship before proceeding, so I asked a lot of confirmation questions. Another good example of a confirmation question would be, "Didn't you say that all three of your children were born at our hospital?" This may provide only incidental information which is a small part of the bigger picture, although it may be crucial if you are asking for a gift to support the pediatric unit.

- **New Information Questions.** These are the cousins to confirmation questions. They allow you to update information and fill in the gaps. To formulate new information questions, I merely ask myself, "What don't I know about this prospect?" Once again, you're not even sure if and how you will use the specific information from a given question. But you want all of the information you can garner as you seek to match the prospect's values with your organization. I like to ask a lot of questions about family history and how someone first interconnected with the organization I represent, so I formulate a lot of new information questions along these lines.

- **Attitude Questions.** These are questions of great importance because they begin to reveal motivational triggers. Attitude questions are typified by phrasing such as, "What is your opinion of . . .," or "How do you feel about . . . ." Attitude questions identify personal needs, values and priorities.

- **Commitment Questions**. Commitment questions tend to come late in the process. These are questions designed to help you locate where you are in the gift decision-making process. Of course, the ultimate type of commitment question would be, "Am I correct in my understanding that I should finalize the

statement of understanding for your $100,000 gift?"
The more common variety would be.

> Should I arrange for a visit with Dr.
> Trafalger so that you may see first hand
> the benefits of her marvelous research?

Another possibility would be,

> Why don't we arrange another visit dur-
> ing which I could illustrate for you how a
> scholarship fund in your name would op-
> erate? That might prove helpful to you as
> you consider your options.

A commitment question might even be in the form
of an invitation to an event or activity. The point is,
you are testing to see how far along you are in the
relationship building process. You want to know how
much interest or involvement you have generated. I
recommend that you formulate these questions very
carefully and think out the precise wording because
it is important for you to receive some clear signals.

In *Major Account Sales Strategy* by Neil Rackham there
is an interesting discussion of why questions are so helpful to
a fund raiser. Why is it that we so strongly recommend you
develop a typology for questions and that you assiduously seek
to ask them during the cultivation process? Here are a few
possibilities:

- *Questions reveal needs.*
- *Questions expose problems.*
- *Questions reveal values.*
- *Questions reveal motivational triggers.*
- *Questions reveal strategic information.*
- *Questions control the discussion.* Have you ever
  noticed how questions can control the flow and
  tempo of a discussion? There have been times when

I have lost control of a discussion because the prospect was such a good questioner and had me responding according to his or her agenda. That's fine and certainly not threatening to me, but eventually I need to redirect the flow of communications. I do this by responding to a question with a question of my own. I'm not interested in controlling, but it is important for me to accomplish my objectives. Questions make that possible.

- *Questions are an effective alternative to disagreements.* Try probing a concern rather than refuting it. It's an extremely effective way to stay out of the fray and it calms your prospect through the process of expiation.
- *Questions give you some thinking time.*

You can train yourself to become a more effective active listener. To assist you along these lines, I want to share some tips for asking questions. I thank *Non-manipulative Selling* for some great ideas in this regard. Experiment with some of these tips and you'll find yourself improving your questioning skills.

- *Ask permission to ask questions.* I think this technique works because it makes the prospect feel more in control. It somehow makes the questioning process less intrusive and threatening. "Do you mind if I ask you about . . ." can work wonders in getting your prospects to let down barriers.
- *Start with broad topics, then narrow the focus.* I have found that going from the general to the specific is a very useful approach. Once again, it makes your questions seem less threatening or intrusive. For example, I am often eager to uncover a prospect's Illinois roots and family interconnections, especially as they pertain to my institution. Rather than seem too bold, I often start my questioning by asking about broad family genealogy and migration patterns to

the state of Illinois. I then begin to focus on parents and what they did with the ultimate hope of uncovering my prospect's relationships with parents and siblings. Ultimately, I make the connection with my university.

- *Build on previous responses.* This works every time, but be careful to avoid becoming obvious. Make sure that you insert some declarative statements between questions or reveal something personal about yourself so that the conversation is more than your simply stringing a lot of questions together. With that caveat, I urge you to use this technique because it works. Observe an effective listener and you will inevitably see him or her use previous responses. The technique is simply one of asking a question and then using whatever information is generated to formulate another question. If I ask someone where they were born and they indicate a northern state I might ask them about the cold climate. Alternatively, I could ask what it was like to grow up in that state or how the family migrated to the state. I will even hold some of the responses I receive in a file in my mind to return to later. What a person says gives you wonderful material for the next question, and you can literally go on forever. Once again, be sure to insert some declarative statements and reveal some things about yourself so as to avoid becoming obnoxious. But it is a great technique.
- *Avoid jargon or vernacular.* This is particularly important for major gifts fund raisers with a gift planning background. We need to simplify, not confuse.
- *Explain the reasons for asking sensitive questions.* There are probably not too many occasions when you will be asking highly sensitive questions, but I have found people to be far more open if you first tell them why you need the information. For example, early in my career as a planned gifts fund raiser I kept running into resistance when I would ask people

for their birth date. When you are in your twenties you have no understanding as to why anyone would be sensitive about date of birth. Of course, I fully understand that sensitivity now. The point is, once I started explaining to prospects that I needed the date of birth in order to run deduction calculations I found them being much more open.

- *Phrase your questions so that prospects answer in a positive fashion.* Avoid "You wouldn't consider . . . would you?" You want your prospects headed in a positive direction which galvanizes vision and urgency.
- *Ask what general benefits are desired.* This is a great technique which reveals much about your prospects. Questions along the lines of, "What would you expect if you were a donor to (board member of) XYZ charity?" Asking people about benefits received, expected or not received, especially using other organizations so as not to be apparent, gives you some marvelous insights.

Let's have some fun exploring poor listening habits. From time to time we all suffer from one or more of these. And it may not be critical in a social setting. However, when it comes to our role as fund raiser we must seek accurate and clear information, which means that we need to work on ourselves to improve. Being aware of poor listening habits will help. I find that I can catch myself and correct the problem without difficulty simply because I am more aware. Feel free to add to my list, but here are some obvious undesirable listening habits.

- *You do all the talking.*
- *You interrupt.* My wife likes to point out that this may be a bit of a "guy thing," and it is certainly a habit my family has honed to a fine art. It's amazing to me how few sentences are ever completed when my immediate family gets together. That's okay

around the Thanksgiving turkey, but it is not a good habit for the fund raiser.

- *You avoid eye contact.* Eye contact is important because it demonstrates connection. The avoidance of it is a distraction. At one of our seminars someone pointed out the dangers of eye contact in a certain culture. Someone else then explained what it was like with her culture. The third person said that with some too much eye contact can cause discomfort and that the appropriate "look away" should be practiced. I said that all of this was far too complicated for me. All I know is that you generally need eye contact, at least from time to time, to ensure good communication.

- *You put words in a speaker's mouth.* Sometimes this is attributable to speech or language differences. I have been helped in this regard by a dear friend who suffered from a stroke. His mind remained rapier sharp, but his communication mechanisms were halting. It was tempting to complete sentences for him, but I learned to let him ask me before I did so. The cousin to putting words in someone's mouth is to finish sentences for him or her. This truly detracts from good communication.

- *You put people on the defensive with your style of questioning.* "How could you possibly reach that conclusion?" Is not a good way to put someone at ease.

- *You start to argue before the other person finishes the case.* This is another form of interrupting, and it is sure to make the other person angry.

- *You digress with stories.* We all know people like this. These are people we all try to avoid because they waste our time by digressing. Worse yet, they generally repeat themselves which only serves to heighten the frustration.

- *You overdo feedback.* Too much nodding of the head or too many "uh huh's" will surely drive the other person crazy. After awhile all you can think about is the other person's reaction and how you wish you had the courage to tell him to stop it.

- *You make judgments about people while they speak.* This in one you can surely train yourself to avoid. It is tempting to jump to conclusions about the type of person you are dealing with after only a few minutes of conversation. This blocks communication and inhibits effective relationship building. Try to avoid pop psychology such as "She must have had a tough childhood based on the nervous speaking habit she is exhibiting." People are far too complex for such a simple analysis, and there are many variables which can affect our behavior at any one time. You will be far more effective if you avoid judgments, and you will often be surprised at how different people really are from your initial judgmental impressions.

At the Institute for Charitable Giving we have developed an assessment of listening skills for fund raisers. We know of nothing else like it. It's a marvelous way to test yourself and assess your listening skills. Remember, it is learned behavior so we can always improve. Indeed, we need to constantly seek improvement in this critical area. You should take the test periodically, and it is an excellent tool to share with your staff. The only qualifier is that we want you to consider these skills in a business context. We are all more relaxed in a social setting, and it is certainly not good for us to exercise our skills at the neighborhood barbecue. Have some fun and help yourself by taking our test.

The Fundraiser's Guide to Listening©

INSTITUTE FOR CHARITABLE GIVING

RATING SCALE		TOTAL POINTS	YOUR LISTENING QUOTIENT
Frequency	**Points**	261 to 285	Outstanding—you're great!
Always	5	216 to 260	You're a good listener, but work on those
Almost Always	4		areas that still require attention.
Usually	3	171 to 215	You're a fair listener, but you should work
Sometimes	2		on your weaknesses.
Seldom	1	Below 171	Active listening is an acquired talent—you
Never	-2		should make an effort to improve your skills.

CONCENTRATION   POINTS

1	When I talk with others, my mind is completely absorbed by what they are saying and it doesn't wander.	
2	In a conversation, I hold my comments until the other person is finished talking, even though my comments may have direct relevance to what he or she is saying.	
3	I do not let interruptions, like ringing telephones or people walking by, distract my attention from what the person is saying.	
4	I consistently keep eye contact with the person I'm talking with.	
5	I make certain I avoid the *mind-reading syndrome*. That's where I determine what I believe the person is thinking without listening carefully to what the person is actually feeling and saying.	
6	When I talk with someone, I have a better recollection of what they said as opposed to what I said.	
7	I listen without judging or being critical.	
8	I concentrate on the person's meaning and message rather than how he or she looks.	
9	I make certain not to daydream while someone else is talking.	
10	I concentrate completely on what is being said, even if I am not totally interested.	
11	I can truly say that in most of my conversations, I feel a sincere interest and an inquiring curiosity.	
12	I listen to the other person's view, even if it differs from mine.	
13	I don't stop listening even if I'm fairly certain I know what the other person is going to say	

INSTITUTE FOR CHARITABLE GIVING

ACKNOWLEDGING

14	I build on previous responses by asking follow-up questions to statements just made.	
15	I make certain that the other person knows I am listening by giving brief, encouraging acknowledgments—such as: *I see, really, that's really interesting*, and so forth.	
16	I make it a practice not to interrupt.	
17	In a discussion, clearly more than half of my time is spent in listening rather than talking.	
18	When appropriate, I reinforce and affirm the other's view by restating their position.	
19	I am able to empathize with the person I'm having a discussion with—I can truly tell *where they are coming from.*	
20	I regularly repeat or paraphrase to make certain I understand what the person is feeling and saying.	
21	I really work and think about motivating the other person to talk by demonstrating a physical and mental attentiveness and showing expressions of interest.	
22	I am careful about not sending the wrong non-verbal messages—moving to a closed-body position, impatiently tapping fingers on a desk, and so forth.	
23	I make certain that when the other person is talking and looks at me, what they see is a happy reflective, responsive appearance.	
24	I demonstrate my understanding and caring with my body language—leaning forward, nodding my head in approval, arching my neck, my facial appearance, and so forth. I give every evidence of riveted attention.	

STRUCTURING

25	Prior to a meeting, I establish my objectives and prepare myself to listen.	
26	When I talk with others, I make mental notes of major ideas, key points, and supporting reasons.	
27	I listen for priorities, sequence, and emphasis.	
28	I move from the general to the specific when I am trying to order or organize the speaker's viewpoint or argument.	
29	I ask for clarification or elaboration regarding the speaker's viewpoint—to ensure proper interpretation and complete understanding of the rationale.	
31	I attend to all promised actions, however great or small, following a discussion.	

The Fundraiser's Guide to Listening

RELATIONSHIP BUILDING

31	When I talk with someone, I encourage a two-way flow of communication by asking open-ended questions
32	I let others know that I am trying to understand what they are saying by using phrases such as *Tell me more about that* or *Can you give me an example?*
33	I encourage people to express their true feelings about an issue.
34	I ask people what they expect from a given action or relationship.
35	I seek information that will allow me to understand the speaker's framework and context so that I can properly interpret what I am hearing.
36	I prepare for my meeting in advance by reading, reviewing, and finding out as much as possible about the person I'll be talking with.
37	In a conversation, I clarify, probe, and question.
38	I attempt to gather more information about the other person by asking questions.
39	I work at learning something from each person.
40	I practice regularly to increase my listening efficiency.

SENSITIVITY

41	When I am talking with others I read their body language as well as listen to their words, in order to fully interpret what they are telling me.
42	In effective listening, the non-verbal communication the person sends me is as important as the verbal, and I am alert to that—facial expressions, posture, eye contact, tapping fingers, checking the time, a poker face, tight facial muscles, frowning, and so forth.
43	I listen to what the speaker is saying, both verbally and non-verbally.
44	I try not to memorize a conversation but rather absorb the feeling and intent of the message.
45	I listen to more than the words themselves—I hear the emotional tone of the person, the pitch, the subtle variations that might indicate displeasure, and so forth.
46	I try to read what's going on behind their spoken words by asking myself what they might be feeling, why they are saying it, and what is implied by what they say.
47	In a listening mode, I am particularly sensitive to how a person, familiar or not, may feel about being touched—knowing that some people do not like it.

INSTITUTE FOR CHARITABLE GIVING

PERSONAL CONCERNS	
48	Before a conversation with a key person, I make certain my energy level is as high as possible because I know fatigue is a barrier to good listening.	
49	I'm careful about personal habits that may be distracting to the person I'm talking with—chewing gum, biting nails, etc.	
50	I make certain, as much as possible, that the physical environment is appropriate for effective conversation—the music is not too loud, the temperature is correct, and so forth.	
51	I dress in a way and make certain my appearance is such that I do not detract from the conversation.	
52	I care greatly about people and those I meet and talk with can sense that in my listening.	
53	I try to assume a *levelling posture* where my eyes are on a straight line with the person I'm talking with.	
54	I'm careful to avoid anything that provides a negative connotation: raising an eyebrow, looking away, rolling my eyes, behaving restlessly, slumping, drumming my fingers, swishing my foot, and so forth.	
55	I go into an important session knowing the kinds of questions I'm going to ask and the manner in which I will ask them.	
56	If the person has negative feelings about me or the Institution, I do not become defensive.	
57	I attempt to arrange the seating so that the prospect is comfortable and in a manner conducive to direct eye contact and communications.	
58	I love my work and I enjoy life—and I believe this helps make me a better listener.	
	TOTAL:	

6 September 1996

The Fundraiser's Guide to Listening

The authors of *Collaborative Selling* share with us some marvelous lessons about active listening. In a general way, it is vital that we ask ourselves three interrelated questions about the prospect with whom we are dealing. We need to know why the person is conveying a particular message. We then want to determine how he or she really *feels* about the issues at hand. Finally, it is important to understand the motives underlying the message.

Collaborative Selling also recommends that you use the funnel approach to active listening. What they mean by that is that you should move from the broad to the narrow and build on previous responses. Where necessary, you should clarify and ask the prospect to expand on something he or she said before. Then it is time to direct the conversation to the next topic.

There are some other steps and techniques I recommend for you to become an effective active listener. In no particular order they are as follows:

- *Concentrate by focusing attention on your prospect — and only on your prospect.*
- *Demonstrate your interest and attention by appropriate feedback.* Be careful not to overdo the feedback.
- *Research by asking questions and making statements which elicit responses.*
- *Observe and interpret body language.* Again, don't overdo it with the psychological implications.
- *Organize the information you obtain.*
- *Understand first and seek to be understood second.*
- *Restate what you hear, but avoid repeating.*
- *Match tempo and tone.* By this I do not mean trying to be something you are not. We are capable of sliding tempo and tone up and down a scale, and we should try to reflect our prospect in this regard. I have a friend in Mississippi who is a delight to be around. His tempo and tone is much different than

mine. I marveled at how it took him ten minutes to cross the street because he was asking everyone he saw about their family members. But I have found it enjoyable to slow down a bit to match his pace. I recall a joint call with one of our staff members who couldn't wait to return to the office to tell others how laid back I was. He observed that I only asked a couple of questions and sat back in the chair and relaxed. He found it difficult to believe that such a hard charger was so calm and laconic. While it was a natural although rarely exhibited state, I had to remind myself before the call that this was the tempo and tone preferred by the prospect.

- *Evaluate what is being said, but avoid value judgments.*
- *Seek to understand feeling as well as verbal content.*

You can become a better listener, and it is essential that you continually hone your skills. It may be the most important thing you can do in furtherance of your fund-raising career. It is also a wonderful tool toward greater pleasure if you truly care about people. In fact, one of the nice things about active listening is that it demonstrates to your prospect that you sincerely care. As an anonymous Zen master once said, "I don't care how much you know until I know how much you care."

10

Issues of Importance to the Nonmanipulative Fund Raiser

It is important to me that none of our shared techniques be considered manipulative. An attempt to manipulate prospects reflects an unsound philosophy relative to fund raising. The outcome should be positive for all involved, otherwise the gift shouldn't be made. It's that simple.

It's also true that manipulative techniques just aren't very effective in major gifts fund raising. Research shows that high pressure works better with decisions of lesser consequence. For gift decisions of lesser magnitude sometimes it's less difficult to say "yes" than to argue. That is not true of a major gift decision and, therefore, pressure is much less effective.

Some research has also been conducted concerning closing techniques. You know what I'm talking about. It's where you say something like, "Would you prefer making your gift in cash or appreciated securities?" which is the type of question designed to provide only a limited menu of answers you desire. What research and experience tell us is that those techniques also tend to be less effective with more sophisticated buyers and bigger proposals. That pleases me because I find those types of tools to be an anathema anyway.

We should continue to measure ourselves as professional fund raisers relative to some very high standards. Tony Alessandra and Rich Berrara in *Collaborative Selling* provide us with some good tests along these lines. We want to distinguish between collaboration and the forcing of solutions or decisions. The questions are rhetorical, but they provide an excellent personal litmus test. It is also well to revisit the list of questions from time to time to ensure that your compass is pointed in the right direction. If you really want to test your mettle in terms of relationship fund raising, ask yourself the following questions:

- Do you think in terms of gifts or in terms of relationships?
- Do you try to win or do you try to help?
- Do you present or do you involve and facilitate?
- Do you impose or do you elicit solutions?
- Do you avoid or ignore issues or do you work to solve issues?
- Do you put your donors' interests first?
- Do you ensure satisfaction even if there is no more giving potential?

The wrong response to some of these questions from time to time does not mean that we are manipulative fund raisers. What it does mean is that we should resolve to do better the next time. Sometimes the pressure to secure a gift, especially one of impressive magnitude, leads us to push too hard. These questions will serve as a reminder of how we need to act if we are to represent our institutions appropriately.

This topic is important to me, foremost because of my philosophy of life. I love people too much and have too much respect for my institution to approach fund raising in other than a collaborative frame of mind. What is nice about this is that in the long run I believe you will be more effective as a major gifts fund raiser if you espouse this philosophy. In my mind, the giving relationship must be built on a foundation of trust and mutual agreement. If two people really wish to effect a gift outcome, the details will not stand in the way. I have observed that prospects like to make their own decisions. The imposition of outcomes leads to resentment. It is certainly true that our donors give because they feel understood, not because of an organizational need. **A true professional will be known by the way he or she conducts business, not by the business he or she is in.** It is vital that we conduct business in the proper manner.

I earlier mentioned *Sales Effectiveness Training*, written by Zaiss and Gordon. One of their topics is building true partnerships. That is exactly what we must do with our donors — build a partnership. If you look at the characteristics of an effective partnership, the first thing you notice is an interdependent nature. You enter into the partnership to begin with because you choose not to or are unable to do something on your own. Therefore, each person is dependent on the other. This certainly holds true in the good giving relationship.

Another characteristic of an effective partnership is a commitment on the part of each to meeting the needs of the other person.

Third, a partnership means a commitment to generate a result which is bigger than the individuals themselves. Remember the business catch phrase of some years ago, "synergy"? It's a good term if not overused. True collaboration with a donor produces synergy. If we do our jobs well, the donor benefits far beyond the value of the gift conveyed as does the institution.

Finally, partnerships have a future. They are more than just a one time deal. I believe this philosophy is extremely important in major gifts fund raising because to adopt it means that we understand the circularity of the process. When a gift is made we give our donors the satisfaction to which they are entitled and use that as a building block to the next gift. The relationship continues and all involved are enriched because that is so.

Zaiss and Gordon are careful to point out the fallacies of the win/lose approach. Let us build on those principles to contrast manipulative gift closing with a true win-win approach.

Manipulative Gift Closing	**Collaborative Win-Win**
Prospects are seen as malleable, able to be manipulated or controlled.	Prospects are viewed as self-directing.
Fund raiser seeks to use information about prospect or use techniques to get prospects to reach a decision.	Fund raiser wishes to help prospects reach decisions of their own based on their needs and desires.
Fund raiser employs strategies and tactics to push the process toward closure.	Fund raiser is a facilitator helping the prospect through the decision making process.
Fund raiser determines prospect's style or typology.	Fund raiser avoids stereotyping or diagnosing.
Fund raiser seeks control.	Fund raiser seeks to understand.
The language of control is utilized.	Collaborative and facilitating language is used.

Major gifts fund raisers should view themselves as gift consultants. The idea is to establish an atmosphere which is conducive to the prospect moving toward a decision whether or not to tender the gift. Our planning and strategizing is designed to link shared values and to create an outcome personally satisfying to the donor's objectives. Control and pressure serve only to create resistance and obstacles, whereas our emphasis must be on creating value.

We must develop a personal philosophy about the kind of fund raiser we wish to be. Obviously, there is a "bottom line" to what we do and we should be measured by results. But all of us must take a stand in life in terms of the kind of person we seek to be and how we go about achieving the sought for results. In my mind, the collaborative mode is both effective and philosophically more acceptable. Once we develop an underpinning philosophy we are in a position to consider more specific attributes of an *effective* major gifts fund raiser.

Once again, I turn to my friend and colleague, Jerold Panas. His book, *Born to Raise*, is not only a wonderful read, but it is very instructive relative to our task in life. Panas interviewed some of the most successful fund raisers in the world. He asked his fund raisers and others with whom they had contact to rank criteria considered important to the success of these outstanding individuals. It is interesting to me that impeccable integrity and being a good listener ranked first and second. No surprise there. Nor is it much of a surprise to consider the next eight factors. They were: ability to motivate; hard worker; concern for people; high expectations; love the work; high energy; perseverance and presence. We can probably all agree that those factors are of importance.

Some of the other shared attributes of the people described in *Born to Raise* are a bit more of an enigma. While I am not sure there is always a direct line between cause and effect, I am positive that the top factors just enumerated are important. At any rate, it is a delight to read *Born to Raise* and a useful thought provoker for any fund raiser. I urge that you add it to your library.

My list of attributes of the successful major gifts fund raiser is far more mundane than the one Panas provides, although there is much overlap and agreement. In no particular order, I think the following characteristics are of importance:

- *Ability to plan and organize;*
- *Oral communications skills;*

- *Written communications skills, especially the ability to simplify the complex and relate it to the prospect's priorities;*
- *Human relations understanding and skills;*
- *A sincere donor orientation;*
- *Achievement motivation and initiative;*
- *Persistence;*
- *Tolerance for deferred gratification;*
- *The ability to recover from a "no";*
- *Self-assurance;*
- *Maturity;*
- *Commitment;*
- *Follow through;*
- *Tolerance for ambiguity; and*
- *Commitment to the institution you serve.*

And when you master the foregoing list, you can sail across other horizons in your spare time.

If you haven't spent time with the book, *The Fifth Discipline* by Peter Senge, I think you would find it instructive. Senge talks about achieving a high level of personal mastery, which translates into a special level of proficiency. I think it's helpful for us to seek that plateau as major gifts fund raisers. Senge observes that people who achieve a high level of personal mastery display a special sense of purpose, a vision that is a calling. Current reality is seen as an ally, not an enemy. In addition, these people have learned how to perceive and work with forces of change rather than resist them.

Senge also found that people of accomplishment are deeply inquisitive, and while they are connected to life and to other people, they maintain their uniqueness as human beings. These are the people who are continually in the learning mode and who view their journey as a process. Learning is a life long quest, and the highly accomplished individual never arrives. As Robert Louis Stevenson said, ". . . to travel hopefully is a better thing than to arrive."

People with a high degree of personal mastery are acutely aware of their own ignorance, shortcomings and growth areas. And yet, somehow, they are deeply self-confident.

By the way, Senge points out that personal development (i.e., family life) is critical to any individual achieving full potential. Sacrificing your family for your job is not the answer.

Finally, an interesting observation is that people with a high degree of personal mastery do not find it necessary to consciously integrate reason and tuition. Mastery is achieved naturally as a by-product of a commitment to utilizing all available resources.

You will find in the *Fifth Discipline* an interesting discussion of possible attitudes toward a vision or an idea. This typology is a useful way for fund raisers to evaluate themselves and their commitments to the mission of the organizations they represent. I also think it is a good way to think about our prospects and the degree to which they may be committed to a particular opportunity. The possible attitudes I refer to are the following:

- **Commitment**. This is where someone believes totally in the premise and will do whatever it takes to make it happen.
- **Enrollment**. This is where someone would like to see the basic objectives accomplished and will do everything to achieve it "within reason."
- **Genuine Compliance**. The person believes or agrees with the premise, but he or she is not a roaring advocate.
- **Formal Compliance**. This is where someone will go along because it's expected, but this person is generally not a staunch believer.
- **Grudging Compliance**. In this case, the person does not share the belief or vision but goes along to the extent necessary.
- **Noncompliance.**
- **Apathy.**

If you were to ask a management consultant about key traits that distinguish those with leadership skills, regardless of endeavor, you would likely find the following items mentioned.

- The leader displays excellence in his or her field.
- The leader demonstrates self-knowledge.
- The leader is a strategic thinker.
- The true leader has the ability to build relationships with others.
- In the true leader there is demonstrated a willingness to help and the ability to teach others.
- The leader desires to learn continually.
- The leader demonstrates effective written and oral communication skills.

It is noteworthy that so many disparate sources agree upon the basic attributes required for success. I think that tells us something. Either we're all going down on the ship together, or there really is something to all of this.

The Harvard Business School undertook a study to determine why certain sales people are successful. An earlier study by the insurance industry revealed only two attributes: a burning desire to succeed and empathy. The problem is that so many different personality types are equally successful in selling or fund raising that finding the common threads can be tricky at best. There is always the danger of falsely concluding that a simple correlation is really cause and effect. The Harvard study sought to dig beneath the surface.

One of the most encouraging things about the Harvard study was it concluded that most people could become top salespeople, or fund raisers presumably, if there is a willingness to study, concentrate and focus. Here are the key attributes for the accomplished salesperson according to the Harvard Business School research. I contend that they are equally applicable to the major gifts fund raiser.

1. You do not take "no" personally. You may be disappointed with a "no," but you are never devastated.

You have high enough levels of confidence and self-esteem to compensate for disappointments.

2. You completely accept responsibility for results achieved. As a corollary to this, you make negatives work to your advantage.
3. You display above average ambition and desire to succeed.
4. You display a high level of empathy.
5. You are intensely goal oriented.
6. You have above average determination and self-discipline.
7. You are impeccably honest.
8. You have the ability to approach strangers, even when uncomfortable.

I was sitting in a hotel room one evening contemplating what I was going to say to a group of fund raisers assembled for one of our Institute for Charitable Giving seminars. The presentation was to be the keynote designed to stimulate some reflection prior to the intense training to begin the following morning. I started thinking about why it is we sometimes fall short as fund raisers. On occasion, the negative viewpoint is a dramatic way to express those things which are of importance to our success. I developed a list of reasons why we sometimes fall short as fund raisers. Here is what I came up with for our assembled group.

- **We sometimes fall short because we fail to make cultivation or solicitation calls.** "Call reluctance" is a common ailment. Sometimes we fail to make the right calls. In other words, stewardship calls are easier to initiate than are cold calls, even though the latter may be far more important to our future success.
- **We sometimes fall short because of poor time management and a failure to focus on priorities.**

- **Sometimes we fail to ask for the gift when we should.**
- **We underachieve when we fail to use volunteers when we should or when we utilize our volunteers improperly.**
- **We will not achieve our potential if we fail to care enough to train ourselves and learn about the dynamics of our business.**
- **We will suffer as fund raisers if we fail to understand our donors.** Empathy and active listening once again enter the picture.
- **We will surely fall short if we fail to understand the concept of mission directed cultivation**. Cultivation is more than mere entertainment, and we must always establish objectives for our fund raising activities.
- **We will fall short if we fail to put our donors' interests first.**
- **Some fund raisers underachieve because of a lack of passion for the cause represented.** If that's the case, it's time to find another organization.
- **And finally, we fall short as professional fund raisers when we fail to understand that the joy of giving is the key to the good giving experience.**

It seems to me that a very clear pattern emerges. The only thing I would add to all of this is that I think the element of sympathy is just as important as empathy. I suppose you can survive very nicely in major gifts fund raising if you do not really like people but you understand them. However, I'm naive enough to believe that you will be even more successful if you truly care for the individuals you deal with. I am also convinced that eventually most people know and sense whether or not you care. Certainly, there is no greater business in the world than major gifts fund raising if you truly love people and want to be associated with important outcomes.

I came across a fascinating word, "entelechy." It means the becoming actual of what was potential. It's a word which traces its origins to Aristotle who would have described it as the condition of a thing whose essence is fully realized. In some philosophies, entelechy is a vital force urging toward self-fulfillment. If we truly care about the missions of our organizations, it is up to us to continually seek to fully realize our potential or essence. This should motivate and charge our every effort.

Finally, the most important part of our quest should be to maintain our standards and to fully realize the essence of the kind of person we seek to be. Let's never forget what Ralph Waldo Emerson told us: "What lies behind us and what lies before us are tiny matters compared to what lies within us."

11

The Care, Nurturing and Training of Boards, Volunteers and Advisory Groups

W hen I first began my development career, training in the use of volunteers was considered critical. Much if not most of fund raising was volunteer driven. Certainly, that's still very true in the early stages of a campaign. After all, you need as much influence as possible from peers who are giving sacrificially to secure those vital early commitments. Volunteers are also used extensively in the broad-based phases of a campaign when it is necessary to have as many troops as is humanly possible making calls in order to reach the masses anchoring the bottom of the giving pyramid.

I'm afraid, however, that for many organizations the utilization of volunteers is becoming a lost art. As mentioned earlier in the book, staff driven solicitations have become common at some organizations simply because it takes time to train volunteers. I suspect that only a handful of organizations have been very effective at training volunteers. Some of the best organizations in terms of volunteer leadership are the various Jewish federations, and we could all learn from their successes. However, even the Jewish federations recognize that volunteers have not been trained in the major gifts process very well, and that is something which needs to be addressed. Some of Gary Tobin's donor surveys reveal this dynamic. Our donors are telling us that they feel underprepared for the task of volunteer fund raising. We can all improve in this regard.

It's interesting to consider the reasons cited for volunteering in a recent survey. In descending order of importance, volunteers indicate that they are motivated by the following factors:

1. A desire to help others.
2. Volunteering is an enjoyable activity.
3. A sense of duty or obligation.
4. The family directly benefited from the organization being assisted.
5. Peer pressure.

In many cases, the recruitment of volunteer leadership may be the key to maximizing our major gifts fund raising success. Certainly, it is often the key to the success of a given campaign. Therefore, a volunteer recruitment strategy, especially for those serving at the highest levels, is essential. It merits great attention. When recruiting volunteers for high level positions you need to consider using peers and organizational officers in order to apply leverage and to meet psychological expectations. You should never take anything for granted.

There is a protocol when recruiting high level volunteers. They are used to dealing with people at the highest level, and they deserve the respect that high level attention imparts. I have observed volunteers recruited for board membership by development staff, and the outcome has usually been a polite declination. I am absolutely convinced that these individuals would have accepted had they been accorded the appropriate treatment and been approached by the CEO of the organization or a significant peer from *the* board. The point is to develop your strategies for volunteer recruitment in the same manner as you would for major gift solicitation. It is that important.

Let me share with you an important aside about volunteer recruitment. It's a lesson I learned the hard way. Specifically, when you recruit for leadership positions be very clear to include giving expectations in the discussion. Whenever you are seeking board membership, whether an advisory committee or *the* board, you should be clear that giving at an appropriate level and participating in the development process is expected. Where the recruitment is for a specific campaign, you should include the solicitation of a specific gift with your request for service. What you wish to avoid is someone assuming a leadership position without giving commensurately. Others "scale down" their giving from the benchmark established by those with the greatest capability. An intention to secure their gift after involving them in the effort seldom operates properly. It is also a mistake to assume that others don't notice what the leaders are giving. It is essential to make sure that giving expectations are coupled with an agreement to commit time.

Some of the reasons we use volunteers include the following:

- *Volunteers legitimize the cause.* By their very presence on a board or committee, high-level volunteers give legitimacy to our mission. They encourage participation because of their standing in the community. Further, the fact that they volunteer for the organization implies that it is well managed in furtherance of the mission, and we have already explored why that is compelling to prospective donors.
- *Volunteers expand staff capabilities.* On one hand, it does take a great deal of effort to train and prepare volunteers. It can be well worth the effort, especially where the payoff is so dramatic as in the early stages of a campaign. But using volunteers can be crucial for the broader-based effort because there would be no other way to reach all of our prospects effectively. Each person taking five prospects, for example, allows us to reach out to prospective donors in a personal way.

- *Volunteers are uniquely capable of assisting in the identification of prospective donors.* This is especially so where we are dealing with the ten percent who are capable of giving ninety percent. We are all familiar with the process of peer review and rating, and this is a key role for volunteers. Whether in the group setting often used for campaigns, or in my preferred mode of one-on-one, volunteers can be of immeasurable assistance in the process of identification and qualification.

- *Volunteers are marvelous at cultivation.* They can bring legitimate enthusiasm and credibility to the entire process. They are also extremely effective at opening doors and ensuring acceptance of invitations to cultivational activities. Securing involvement and gaining access may be as elusive as the gift itself. Volunteers help bridge that gap between our world and the prospect's.

- *Volunteers are often our most effective solicitors.* Once again, volunteers can provide peer influence or leverage. While we know there is a cut off point in terms of what a prospect will donate simply because a peers asks, there is nonetheless great leverage when a peer solicits someone of the same status for a like commitment. Obviously, this implies the very important principle of the solicitor having made an appropriate commitment prior to seeking gifts from others. Volunteers bring legitimacy to the solicitation process. Certainly, volunteers have the ability to say things that staff cannot when soliciting a gift or when responding to an objection.

It is important that we recognize the many possible roles played by volunteers. We often think in terms of our primary board. But there are advisory committees, foundation boards, and committees or personal involvement with projects of limited duration. We should also think of our volunteers in terms of playing roles as centers of influence, natural partners and primary players.

There are some sound principles worth following when it comes to managing our volunteers and their various roles. My list would include:

- *The busiest, most successful person will usually be the best volunteer.* It is often the case that we do not seek the involvement of these individuals because of our concern about their busy schedules. And let's be realistic, some organizations will be unable to recruit volunteers at the very highest levels. That is just fine. Those warm, wonderful and capable people in the "next tier," however you define that, will be just as successful. Although, you should never avoid seeking volunteer involvement because of a presumption about time. You don't know unless you ask.

- *Always place your volunteers in positions to be successful, and make sure that the expectations of a given call are fully explained.* Keep in mind that I consider the high level administrators of our organizations to be volunteers. I say this because they have a right to be trained, nurtured and prepared just as our lay volunteers. We need to be very careful to use these important people in ways which maximize their opportunity for success. After all, these people are used to being placed in positions of success. That doesn't mean, however, that you cannot take a volunteer on a speculative or cold call. What is essential in those cases is to make sure that the expectations of the call are fully explained. Depending upon the volunteer, I've had little difficulty in situations where we failed to achieve the objective but knew that might well be the case. Where you really get yourself into trouble is when you fail to clearly articulate the possibilities. This is especially true where a volunteer's confidence is somewhat tenuous or fragile.

- *It is important that we be as professional in our behavior as our volunteers are in their particular business or profession.* Gone are the days where the "brothers and sisters of the poor" approach is either expected or effective. Remember that we are the tangible substitutes for our organizations. Prospective donors and volunteers are impressed by well managed organizations whose aspirations they share. Let's also remember that it is important to convey to our prospective volunteers that we will use their time judiciously. For many of the highest level volunteers, giving time is even more difficult than giving resources. If we convey and indicate that we will use their time judiciously, and a professional approach sends a strong signal in that regard, we will stand a better chance of success.
- *Be clear about giving expectations associated with the volunteer position.*
- *Also be clear about the time expectations associated with accepting the position.* Experience shows that merely associating a powerful volunteer's name with the cause is ineffectual. Better to involve a committed volunteer at the next level. I have found it effective to say to the highest level volunteer-prospects that we will be careful and judicious in the use of his or her time. However, there are some meetings and activities for which their presence is crucial, and it is important that they be a part of them to the extent possible. I further indicate that I will always be quite clear in differentiating between the less important and more important activities. Once again, this approach conveys the professionalism we know is important to the process.
- *Good volunteers are successful people.* Don't use them unless there is a good reason. In other words, be careful to think out your objectives. Merely seeking their involvement with unclear or muddled objectives hardly conveys professionalism and is quickly

noticed by these bright individuals. Further, don't expect accomplished people to be "shrinking violets." If you are not seeking advice, then don't call the group an advisory committee. Further, where you do seek input don't be surprised if it is conveyed in an assertive manner. Good volunteers will not always agree with you, nor will they always understand the process. You can be sure that they will not be shy about expressing themselves, and you must be prepared to handle that. Just be sure of your professional positions and don't feel compelled to back down from what you know to be the correct approach.

• *Involvement is more important than informing.* Find a pretext to truly involve a volunteer and your are light years ahead. Even if it is involvement in a limited duration project or you are seeking focused advice, you can advance your position by doing more than simply "keeping someone posted."

• *Take care of the details with your volunteers because the small things can undermine your success.* I am not a particularly good detail person, but I have trained myself to try to think of everything when it comes to my volunteers. Once again, the issue of professionalism arises. High level volunteers are used to staff members who think of details and ensure good experiences. We must be prepared in all respects by providing them with information, materials and background.

• *Our volunteers must contribute before they solicit others.* This, as mentioned earlier, is one of my inviolate rules.

• *The volunteer always gets the credit.* If it bothers your ego to see other people take credit for your efforts, strategies and accomplishments, then perhaps you need to find another profession. It is useful and proper that our volunteers (also our high level administrators) receive the credit for a positive gift outcome and step into the limelight when the major event is announced. This is because it conveys to our donors how important they are to the organization. It is also appropriate because of the way it positions the organization in the public's mind. Your satisfaction as a fund raiser must come from the outcome and from seeing your volunteers step forward to accept a wonderful gift. Most importantly, our satisfaction will come from witnessing our donors receiving the pride, prestige and satisfaction to which they are entitled. It was a privilege for me to have spent several years working very closely with a university president who was both a dynamic decision maker and an effective fund raiser. After pretty much closing one gift of significant magnitude, I suggested that he call on the prospects to finalize everything. With good humor he wryly observed, "I know you're sending me there because I'm such an effective gift closer. Somehow, I think the deed has already been done and I'm going in to gather up the credit." To a certain extent, he was correct. However, it was the appropriate thing to do for the donors because of their great respect for the president and his position. It is also true that we might not have secured the gift in the first place without the president's earlier involvement. At any rate, the volunteer gets the credit.

- *The "rule of thirds" applies to most volunteer situations.* You know the rule. It says that one-third of your volunteers will be effective, and the second third will follow that lead and contribute. The final one-third will be relatively inert. Somehow, it just seems to work that way.

Let's now turn our attention to boards. I speak here of any type of board, whether advisory or governing. Indeed, you may well deal with more than one board. Independent foundation boards and advisory committees are often formed because we need a collection of individuals with the appropriate attributes if we are to maximize our fund-raising success. In some settings, there is no other choice but to organize around the primary governing board. For example, at state assisted universities, trustees are often elected or appointed by the governor. There is no way they will have those attributes of giving and getting that are necessary for effective fund raising. You need to find another mechanism.

Consider what John W. Pocock, a prolific writer about boards, observed. He urged that your board, whether advisory or governing, be structured with fund raising in mind. You need leaders, askers, cultivators and identifiers. Of course, where these attributes are wrapped together in a single individual you are at an advantage. Pocock stated that board members must create positive awareness of the organization through advocacy. They should also be involved in identifying private gift opportunities. The board must help realistically access the feasibility of fund-raising goals, often with the assistance of professional counsel. As it relates to fund raising, it is the board's responsibility to see it that the development function is well organized under the day to day leaders who "call the shots." They must also ensure adequate budgeting.

Pocock described what individual board members must do. On his list were the following:

- *Give money.*
- *Assess and apply their skills in fund raising as the staff may request.* Fund raisers should keep in mind that not all board members are effective or willing askers.
- *Individual board members should be open to training in fund raising.* There are too many "experts" in Pocock's mind, and board members should be receptive to learning. As a matter of fact, the research earlier noted indicated that they are probably eager for such training if we urge it upon them.
- *Individual board members are urged by Pocock to listen to their development staff and let the staff*

guide their efforts. He warns against micro-management of the fund-raising process.

Francis Pray has been a long-time observer of the fund raising equation as it relates to boards. He likes to refer to a study which concluded that all of the effective organizations under examination had an unusually involved and successful board. No surprise there. Pray commented, "I have never known a truly successful fund-raising effort that was not at some point supported effectively by the board." Amen.

Theodore Chase, a volunteer leader in the Boston area, elaborated on Pray's general premise. He said,

> Knowledge and commitment on the part of individual board members are essential if the board is to provide leadership in development, but enthusiasm is equally important.

When asked about the attributes of an effective volunteer board I like to build on the old aphorism of "giving and getting." Actually, I think that observation may be a bit too cute for some people. You have probably also heard of the three W's, Wealth, Wisdom and Work. My friend Jerry Panas likes to add a fourth — Wallop. All of these statements make a valid point, but I like to carry it to the next step. I would cite such things as a natural relationship to the organization; affluence and/or influence relative to the task; a willingness to contribute at the appropriate level; a strong interest in the organization; an ability and willingness to communicate to others concerning the organization's case for support; and a sense of urgency about the organization's mission.

Thomas Broce's enumeration of qualities of good board members reinforces the list just provided, but it is considerably more compelling and complete. Broce cites these attributes:

- A good board member has a strong relationship with or interest in the organization being served.
- The effective board member brings affluence or influence to the equation.

- An effective board member demonstrates and acts upon a willingness to contribute at a level appropriate to his or her capabilities.
- A good board member has enough interest to ask to right questions and to challenge the staff.
- An effective board member demonstrates a willingness to communicate with others concerning his or her belief in the organization. In other words, the desired board member is an enthusiastic advocate.
- The good board member has a willingness to stay informed about the organization.
- Effective board members demonstrate a sense of urgency about the organization's mission.

When I make presentations to boards about fund raising I like to emphasize a few key points. These are usually well received.

- **Fund raising can be enjoyable.** Charge your staff with preparing you well, and then enjoy it because you are offering people an opportunity to gain great satisfaction and further a cause of importance.
- **Try not to be offended when you are guided by the professional.** It is more of an art than a science, so sometimes your judgment about a given strategy or situation should prevail. However, an effective professional, and that is the only type you wish to have serving your organization, will be assertive about sound fund-raising principles and approaches. Challenge, but be open to guidance.
- **Don't think the fund-raising task is "too rich for your blood."** If you contribute at the appropriate level, that will send the needed message.
- **Don't put fund raising off onto others.** Board involvement is essential and cannot be delegated. Play willingly and enthusiastically your role as natural partner, primary player and informed advocate.

I have found what Tobin discovered in his surveys. Specifically, volunteers are receptive to solicitation training. It might prove instructive for me to share with you those things which we tell our volunteer solicitors. Obviously, this is done in the context of a much more elaborate discussion of the various principles. Even a bit of role playing can be valuable. Here are some of the messages which should be conveyed to your volunteer solicitors.

- *Make your sacrificial gift first.*
- *Know your prospect's reasons for giving.* In other words, consider the appealing benefits of the project from your prospect's vantage point.
- *See the prospect in person.*
- *Use your own gift to help persuade.*
- *Ask for a specific amount.*
- *Ask for a specific purpose.* Even if the gift is unrestricted, be specific such as discussing a named endowment fund or highlighting in human terms the outcomes to be achieved by the unrestricted support.
- *Listen and use silence to your advantage.*
- *Have in mind answers to commonly raised objections.*
- *Don't accept a lesser gift too soon.* Allow time for the proposition to be considered by the prospect and only go to a lower cost alternative where it is mandatory. It is better to come back another day to discuss a lower level commitment because in the interim the prospect may find a way to achieve the opportunity first tendered.
- *Don't lose a prospect because he or she won't give now.* Continue to cultivate.
- *Don't go to the gift spread too soon.* Mention optional payment schedules only if it will help in the decision making process. It is best to first probe to ensure that the gift spread will really help.

- *Do not go to the deferred gift option too soon.* This one is better left as a "trump card" to be played at a later date.

I like to convey to our volunteer solicitors the sage observations of Aryeh Nesher. Nesher observed,

> The greatest weakness among solicitors is the lack of knowledge on how to probe and how to listen. They are so eager to tell more, that when the prospect talks they're thinking "What do I say next?"

Finally, Nesher summed up the process nicely when he stated, "People don't like to be solicited. Don't solicit them. People like to give gifts. Help them to give."

Peter Drucker, the famed management guru, was good enough to attend one of our seminars. There were about 100 fund raisers and volunteers/board members in attendance. Drucker inquired of the audience as to how many were board members and volunteers. About 20 percent of the group raised a hand to the sky. Drucker indicated that he lauded their volunteer service and wanted to address their particular role in service of the nonprofit organization.

What Drucker said was very compelling and I took notes furiously. I believe I captured the essence of his message. Drucker said that board members must know why the organization exists. They should face budgets with courage, deficits with dismay and recover quickly from surpluses. He further charged them with developing the ability to interpret the mission of the organization in words of two syllables. Finally, he observed that it would be helpful to combine a New England sense of obligation with an Irish sense of humor.

Drucker went on the enumerate some of the board's roles. He charges boards with the following:

- Articulation of the mission.
- Ensuring long range and strategic planning.
- Ensuring adequate resources, which at least partially translates into major gifts fund raising.

- Managing resources.
- Determining and monitoring programs and purposes.
- Serving as the ultimate court of appeal.

With the room hushed, Drucker went on to articulate the true meaning of board membership. He said,

> The board leader represents not only what we are, but above all, what we know the organization should be. Membership on a board is not power, it is responsibility. What I mean by this is responsibility not just to the organization, but to the board itself, to the staff and to the institution's mission.

Drucker was right. Our volunteers and board members must convey to prospective donors what the organization aspires to accomplish in human terms. Thoreau said, "If one advances confidently in the direction of his dreams and endeavors to live the life he has imagined, he will meet with a success unexpected in common hours." Our volunteers and our boards, through their gifts of time and resources, can help our organizations advance confidently in the direction of our dreams. With visionary leadership, we will surely meet with success unexpected in common hours.

12

A Potpourri of Important Issues

Conducting seminars is a wonderful way to learn. I always seem to get more than I give. Of importance to me when I started making such presentations was to encourage a diverse audience. The nonprofit world is rich in its diversity, and I wanted all different types of organizations represented. It is easy to become too insular with our programming, and there is much to be learned by considering the challenges others face. Dealing with sectors other than your own forces you to think "out of the box." Some of the most useful and creative ideas I have secured came from fund raisers representing sectors far different than the one I deal with on a daily basis.

During my seminar presentations I am frequently asked about certain issues which seem to be of importance to us all. I thought this would be a good time for me to share with you some of my thoughts concerning these matters.

Endowment versus
Bricks and Mortar

When I first started in fund raising I was told that raising funds for buildings was far easier than securing gifts for endowment. This seemed logical to me. After all, buildings and the naming opportunities associated with them are tangible. Everyone knows that tangibles are easier to market than intangibles. What I have found, however, is that endowment is actually easier to market than building opportunities.

Let me say from the start that there is no question some of our prospects will be attracted primarily or exclusively to building opportunities. Some people are just psychologically attuned that way. They become excited about physical plant and all that it represents. In those cases, endowment is a hard sell. We are all different, and it is important to probe so that we understand when our prospects are desirous of being associated with a building opportunity.

However, most donors can be excited to endowment opportunities if we package them correctly. Our limitations are self-imposed. Buildings and physical plant package themselves, whereas endowment is sometimes a confusing concept. It was easier to raise money for buildings because we never properly defined endowments for our donors in human terms. This is changing as evidenced by the fact that many campaigns are weighted toward endowment, whereas for years campaigns were highly focused on physical plant.

You will notice that even highly sophisticated donors do not always understand the concept of endowment. We often don't describe it in user friendly terms. I found this barrier falling when I started talking to our donors in terms of a gift the principal of which remains intact with only the income used for the intended purpose. I often say to donors that endowment gifts are, perhaps, the most important type of support they can provide. This is because the principal remains invested and only the annual income is used for the donor's chosen purpose. I further point out that the permanence is important because *every year* there will be meaningful and important support provided for the chosen purposes. I then indicate that the permanence provides us with a nice opportunity to recognize our special friends who are making such a huge difference in the life of the institution and those it serves. When you explain endowment in those terms, it can be quite exciting.

With groups that are just starting an endowment program I begin with the issue of fiduciary policies, such as establishing payout levels and investment approaches. I explain the options and how to analyze them. An examination of the endowment policies adopted by other organizations often helps in that regard. Where I spend the greatest amount of time, however, is in the packaging of endowment outcomes.

During a presentation for Junior Achievement we started discussing the issue of laddering naming opportunities and gearing endowment payout to same. I asked someone how much it might cost to provide a middle school student with a Junior Achievement experience. I rounded the figure upward to reflect overhead, inflation and unknowns. Let us say that the figure comes to $30 per student. If there is an average of 30 students in a class at $30 each it would take $900 per year to fund one classroom. If we assume a five percent endowment payout, with the balance of the investment return being reinvested as principal, it would take $18,000 to name one classroom. We then moved on to discuss the naming of grades, schools and entire school systems. It's almost that easy, and you can also look at what other organizations are doing. We are used to thinking in those terms relative to buildings, wings and rooms, but many of us had never considered how to gear endowment payouts to naming.

I was struck as it regards endowment and naming by a gift I observed during the first campaign at our institution. One of our wonderful donors supported a building program because it was deemed the highest priority, but what really would have excited her was something associated with the fine arts. Of course, the new building she funded was named in her honor, but because of her many gifts we also named a theater which had been built many years ago in her honor. This thrilled her.

I then realized that there was no need to think in a linear fashion. Donors do not trace the serial numbers on the dollar bills they donate, rather they donate for an outcome and what we need to do is to recognize the gift by providing an appropriate naming opportunity. Once we start thinking in this fashion, the marketing of endowment becomes easier. We often consider naming existing wings or rooms to honor an endowment donor even though the dollars are no longer needed for construction. We do this simply because we think it is appropriate to the level of giving and will please the individual involved.

Gift Agreements

Let me share with you one marvelous marketing tool as it pertains to endowment. I refer to what are commonly called gift agreements or statements of understanding. I am not speaking here of pledge agreements. Actually, many organizations seldom use pledge agreements anymore. Personally, I rarely use pledge agreements and only when requested to do so by a donor or when particular circumstances call for it.

Pledge agreements are seldom legally enforceable. Under the law, only when consideration is given, such as constructing a building or committing funds, is a pledge agreement to a charitable organization actually enforceable. Where the project is that major or involves an extensive institutional commitment, a pledge agreement should certainly be considered. In addition to the fact that such a document is not usually legally enforceable, the question becomes one of public policy. If a donor were unable to continue payment on a gift commitment, would it really be wise to take legal action? There may be those rare cases where some action is justified because the institution made a formidable commitment. However, the vast majority of giving situations will not fit that description and there would be much public relations harm from a lawsuit to enforce payment. Sometimes pledges are unpaid because of financial reversals, and that is surely an instance where it makes little sense to pursue a legal remedy. The point that is overriding in my mind is the fact that when properly structured a giving relationship is a partnership. I would not wish to force a donor to make payments on a pledge if he or she no longer wanted to pursue the opportunity.

What is common is to implement a statement of understanding or a gift agreement. There are two sound business reasons for executing such a document. First, it ensures a complete understanding about what is to be accomplished. Second, it guarantees the faithful administration of an endowment fund, and this is of understandable importance when you are dealing with perpetuity.

This last issue prompted me to suggest to my foundation that all endowment gifts, whether current or deferred, be covered by some sort of fund agreement. After all, as fiduciaries it represented sound practice. I was tired of the lack of documentation in our files concerning how gifts were to be used. The existing information was often incomplete as to a donor's specific preferences about the operation of an endowment, and in many cases there was no documentation at all. You can imagine the internal squabbling this led to. We have three campuses, and if a gift were left for engineering the two different deans laid claim to the funds. We settled that by opting for the college from which the donor graduated, but we still had far too many arguments to suit me. We owed it to our donors to be good business people, and the fund agreement seemed to be the perfect answer.

This is where legal counsel became involved and our fund agreement ended up being quasi-legal in nature. It in no way bound a prospective donor to a gift, but it did ensure that when contributions were received they were put to the intended use. It also gave us an opportunity to become as detailed as the donor wished relative to the operation of a given fund. The fund agreement could then be referenced in deferred giving documents or in letters of gift conveyance. In summary, it was an excellent business decision.

What I later found, however, was that these fund agreements had another, more important use. I discovered that it made an intangible (endowment) into a tangible ("my fund"). Fund agreements became a way to involve donors in the gifting process and increase their stake in a possible gift. Fund agreements encouraged prospects to gently cross a psychological line and begin developing their own outcomes. How wonderful!

I now use fund agreements very early in the process. I often stamp "draft" on the agreement and share it with a prospect early in the discussions. I explain that it is an example of what could be accomplished. In a sense, the prospect helps you write his or her own proposal. Once the language is finalized, we have all appropriate parties sign and we provide the donor with a copy. Now the endowment fund is really tangible. I even discovered some donors showing the fund agreement to friends as an example of an important accomplishment. In recognition of our discovery of the psychological benefits, we developed a cover for our fund agreements. We also added signatories at increasing levels of authority commensurate with the magnitude of the gift. For example, with an endowed chair we have a fund agreement signed by the chancellor or president.

All I am really saying is that some sort of fund agreement or statement of understanding can help render endowment opportunities more tangible. The quasi-legal form works well for us because it implies that everything is quite official and important. However, other forms may work equally as well. I observed one organization that had a statement of understanding which enumerated the use of the gift without all of the legal descriptions and definitions. This language was put on parchment paper which contained some sort of official seal. I am sure that donors to this organization feel as if they are accomplishing something important when they sign.

I remember with fondness a telephone call I received from a representative in our business office. She asked that I admonish one of our staff members about fund agreements. She said that this particular fund raiser was inserting a lot of additional information which was extraneous to the fiduciary administration of the fund. I asked about the nature of this superfluous information. I was told that the fund raiser included a clause about the purpose of the gift in which he extensively described the donors, their families and their association with our institution. I told our business office representative that she would regret that telephone call because from here on out I was going to do the same thing. What a marvelous idea for further involving prospective donors. This perceptive staff member was right on the mark. I urge you to follow suit with a statement of understanding or gift agreement appropriate to your organization.

Proposal

I earlier observed that proposals aren't really that important to our donors. Many don't even read them. However, there are a couple of suggestions I have that may render proposals more useful.

First, in the body of the proposal I make frequent reference to the particular naming opportunity. Whether a building, wing or endowment fund, I always have this typed in boldface letters. Further, if a building or wing is to be named, I attach to the proposal an artist's rendering with signage displaying the donors' names. Be sure always to use the names of both the wife and husband unless told otherwise by a natural partner.

My second suggestion is to use cover letters signed by important figures. During a campaign some years ago we were lamenting the fact that we had to save our president and campaign chair for a few major solicitations. After all, time was limited and their personal attention was called for only in cases where the gift potential was dramatic. Quite spontaneously it was suggested that we utilize cover letters signed by either or both of these individuals for proposals below the level which merited their personal attention. This was another one of those great ideas!

We started attaching cover letters to our proposals from our president and campaign chair, which in part read,

> I know that Jack and Denise are visiting with you today about our campaign and a special opportunity. I want to thank you for receiving them and for your consideration of this important matter.

The letter went on to include such things as, "I want you to know of my personal appreciation for you consideration of this most important leadership opportunity." We even began including, "Please feel free to call on me personally if I can ever be of service," although we hoped that offer was not seized on too many occasions. I think that most of our prospects knew that the letter was designed for affect, but they enjoyed it nonetheless. I think any of us would enjoy receiving a personal letter from a person of standing and importance.

Gift Clubs

This section is not intended as a primer on gift clubs. However, I do want to make a few observations.

For the organization just beginning in major gifts I often recommend that a few gift clubs be established. The reason for this is to provide the fund raising team with convenient targets and a rationale for asking for gifts at a certain level. Gift clubs provide their own internal logic. What I mean by this is in response to a prospect asking (and they seldom do), "Why are you seeking a $1,500 commitment?" The answer becomes, "Because that will place you in the Platinum Club, an association I know you will appreciate and enjoy." That's all you really need.

The other nice thing about gift clubs for a fledgling organization is that they give you the means for some immediate successes. I found that there was a void in the advice I was providing organizations. I was preaching the faith about major gifts and rightfully indicating that it might be a few years before results become visible. My colleagues were telling me that the logic was clear and the board understood perfectly, but human nature being what it is they were still were going to be asked at next year's retreat about the results of the major gifts efforts. I hadn't thought about that because I am not measured by sustaining gifts and it had been many years since I had been in the position of building a program.

It became clear to me how we could secure immediate results, thereby satisfying the short term focus, while still nurturing key relationships for major commitments. To reach this realization all I had to do was look at my continuum which runs from sustaining gifts through major commitments to ultimate gifts. I was sure that it would not be very productive to approach major gifts prospects with the following logic:

> I know there is little pre-existing relationship with our organization, but I also know you are capable of a six figure commitment because of what you have done for the museum. Therefore, to save time why don't we get right to our $250,000 proposal.

Try it if you like, but in my experience that doesn't work. However, you can ask a major prospect for a gift below the stop and think level very early on, perhaps even during the first call, and expect some results. This is where gift clubs, with levels below stop and think, are particularly useful for the new organization. For the established program, they can be used in the same way for new prospects, and that is exactly what I do. I seek Presidents Council gifts early in the relationship from prospects capable of seven figure commitments. Obviously, I intend someday to seek support at the appropriate level, but in the meantime I have secured some important funds for my organization. By using the gift club I help provide the donor with a good giving experience and create a context and pretext for further involvement.

If you are just starting, remember that the purpose of a gift club includes providing an early giving target, below stop and think for the 10 percent who can give 90 percent, and it gives you a means of cultivation through involvement in special events. Gift clubs are also a context for recognition, and they generate a modest amount of peer pressure for people to get involved.

What I particularly like are the special events which can be held for gift club members. Every year I am associated with two major activities, quite disparate in content, whereby we honor and recognize our Presidents Council members. It is a wonderful way to cultivate and involve. We also send a subtle message about major gifts fund raising by recognizing, in a very tasteful way, some of our donors who have made especially meaningful commitments during the year.

Finally, I want to share with you a few of my precepts about creating gift clubs, either from scratch or in addition to existing organizations. Of course, there are the two types of clubs, those to recognize sustaining gifts and those for cumulative lifetime giving. We used to worry that the cumulative giving organizations would place a cap on a donor's contribution, but that was quickly dispelled. The gift club is not the sole rational for involvement, and if you provide good stewardship and cultivate effectively, giving begets giving at much higher levels. Experience shows that your problem is more likely to be adding additional clubs at higher levels as a result of your fund raising success.

I always recommend that you place the thresholds a bit higher than your instincts would tell you to do. Also, try to keep it simple in terms of qualification. I think it is fine to have two levels for a cumulative gift club, one for current and another for deferred. The deferred threshold could be some convenient multiple, such as 2.5 times, the outright threshold. However, you should avoid further differentiation between gift types, either in terms of revocability versus irrevocability or the age of the donor. It is not merited and it is too complicated. At the very high levels I wouldn't differentiate between outright and deferred at all. For example, when we established a $1 million donor club I observed that these friends are too committed and important to imply any differences regarding giving method. The method of giving is personal and incidental to each prospect, and they are all equally valid. You can trust me when I tell you that someone will not insert a $1 million provision into his or her estate plan simply to gain access to your prestigious club.

Finally, save your most prestigious names for last as you will surely have a need for gift clubs at a higher level. We took our time in establishing a $1 million club because it wouldn't have been meaningful with only one or two members. Once we had a critical mass, we then proceeded and the challenge was to find an appropriate name. Keep some in reserve for later use.

The Merger of Planned and Major Gifts

I have observed the merger of planned and major gifts of late, and it is about time. I was as guilty as anyone in having this one all wrong for many years. When I first started in the business it was called deferred giving. That implies a gift which is committed now but the use by the organization is deferred. Such things as life income gifts and bequests obviously fit the description of a deferred technique.

Eventually, the operative term became planned giving. My definition of planned giving is the process whereby you plan a gift in light of 1) donor needs and objectives, and 2) prevailing tax law as to maximize the benefit to both the donor and the organization. There are a few things which are important about that definition. It is no mistake that I place first a consideration of the donor's needs and objectives. As I mentioned earlier, our donor's interests must come first. Further, the tax law is a means to an end, which is a benefit for

both the donor and the organization. Note the mutuality implied. If we do our jobs well, the donor gains far more in satisfaction than any economic or tax measurement. Finally, you
will notice that nowhere do I reference a technique. The technique is incidental to the situation and is something to be explored in the context of what will allow the donor to achieve a
shared goal with the organization. Obviously, things do not
always go in a straight line. Sometimes prospects are attracted
to us by the tax savings or the economic benefit, but I always
seek to involve them in an outcome such that I can move
them to a higher motivational plane. All charitable organizations can provide the same tax benefits, but the real gratification from giving is unique to each opportunity and case for
support. The act of giving is simply a means to an end.

All major gifts fund raisers, whether the emphasis is on
deferred or outright, should seek combination commitments
over the long term. It is the logical thing to do when you
consider the progression of a relationship which includes gifts
along the way. I am always seeking the outright gift, and I feel
that if such a commitment is possible at a certain level more
would be possible through a life income arrangement. Still
more is possible through a properly structured estate plan
provision. The technique will be determined by the given situation and stage in life cycle, and it is always an issue of seeking a means to a shared end.

For years those of us in planned giving seemed to feel
that we had to hire technicians. The unfortunate outcome
was that we were hiring many people who were very effective
at developing life income documents and computing deductions, but who were often weak at relationship building and
gift closure. We learned the hard way to emphasize first the
human relationship skills while relegating the technical aspects
to second place. Of course, if someone is going to deal with
deferred gift techniques it is important that he or she have an
aptitude for the technical issues, but more important to their
success will be their ability to build relationships. You can always
secure the technical assistance. I have observed many planned
gift fund raisers who were effective at closing gifts but only

had a modicum of proficiency with the technical nuances. Still, they thrived and their organizations benefited.

As to those fund raisers who are traditionally recognized as specialists in major gifts, I believe there is a certain threshold of knowledge which is necessary if we are to serve our donors properly and seize opportunities. A good major gifts fund raiser does not necessarily want to be a technician, nor is that a necessity. However, it is important to raise issues and open up avenues of discussion. I worked with a major gifts fund raiser who was wonderful at that. He would tell a donor that there might be a planning opportunity with dramatic benefits which would allow for an important gift. He would then state one or two generalities about possible tax savings or an increase in income. When the prospect would ask for details, this fund raiser would say, "I'm not a technician, but I have a friend who is great at this stuff, and why don't we get together next Tuesday to review everything." He was wise enough to pick up the cues and use the information wisely. What was also interesting to observe is that he created another move. In the process he was gaining greater involvement and appreciation on the part of the donor. All major gifts fund raisers should have enough knowledge to seize opportunities in that way.

What I see occurring is a recognition that all of us who deal with the 10 percent who can give 90 percent are major gifts fund raisers. Obviously, some of us may deal disproportionately with prospects with a certain profile because of a background and training in tax planning and charitable giving. However, it's all cut out of the same cloth and the objective is to secure a gift which pleases the donor and serves the institution. Those fund raisers who are not acclimated to the tax aspects can use the more technically oriented professional as a resource or in a joint call representing the next move. It all works very nicely, and it is about time that we recognize the process from the donor's standpoint. The tax and financial aspects are a means to an end and all of us who are embarked on this enterprise are fund raisers.

Prospect Tracking Systems

I am always asked about prospect tracking systems at our seminars. I have a particular philosophy that I like to share. I tried to avoid the subject at first because I long ago recognized that the mechanics of tracking and gift recording systems are too often given the greatest attention. They are often an excuse for inaction. "We can't start our calls yet because our system isn't in place." Many of us with gray hair learned long ago that you can operate very nicely without a system and that how you track prospects is not the most vital consideration.

What I primarily recommend is that you keep your tracking system as simple as possible. In some settings, this is no mean task. I had a very difficult time convincing some systems people that all of the "bells and whistles" simply got in the way. The last thing I wanted was for my staff members to be spending a lot of time at the computer going through prospect strategy screens. I wanted a system that would call up my prospects by classification (i.e., potential level and readiness) and indicate the date of last contact. A phone number would also be helpful. I wanted only a short summary list to take on trips with me, and I wanted to be free of those incredibly cumbersome and heavy printouts. It took me a while to accomplish that because there is always the tendency to keep adding features. Try to resist.

What is essential in any tracking system is to classify prospects by potential and by stage in the cultivation/solicitation process. I provided you with a couple of possible classification systems earlier in the book. You then want the ability to identify vital individuals involved in the process, such as natural partners and primary players. Of course, all prospects should have a designated moves manager. We call this person at our organization the prospect manager, but the title is not what is important.

If you represent a big and complex organization you could consider an additional step. At our institution we have many fund raisers representing colleges and units, and they felt left out when I was assigned a mega prospect, even though I had worked with that person for years. We added a designation called "staff," which means another fund raiser who, under the coordination of the moves manager, plays a role in the cultivation, strategizing and solicitation process.

You should also keep your supporting forms very simple. I refer here to the forms submitted to major gifts committees seeking an assignment, and, more importantly, call reports. Of greatest importance on call reports which support a tracking system are the areas on which to record contacts and describe the next planned contact. You need to include target dates for the next contact. These target dates become your tickler system, whether it is kept manually or is picked up on automatic tracking system. In terms of your call reports, it is vital that you accomplish the following:

- **A description of each move and an indication whether it was a foreground or background initiative.**
- **A brief analysis of each move, including what was learned and observed.**
- **The date of completion of each move.**
- **A target date for the next move.**
- **Comments.**

If an automatic tracking system does not accommodate a description of the strategic considerations, the fund raiser must maintain the information physically.

Finally, to ensure that you use a tracking system properly and to avoid unwieldliness, you should at all costs resist the temptation to duplicate your primary data base relative to biographical or giving data. Of course, it is fine that the systems talk to one another, but you should keep your contact management as fundamental as possible. It should be a tool to free your time for face-to-face contacts.

I hope these observations prove of value to you as you set about the task of maximizing the potential of your major gifts programs. The primary need is for you to make personal calls. When a person of integrity, representing a worthy organization, visits with an individual who cares, great things happen. All of the tools, techniques and tips aside, major gifts fund raisers simply need to get out of the office and make things happen with people who share the vision of the organization. Brian O'Connell aptly described the process as follows:

> Raising money takes dogged persistence, bull headedness, salesmanship, year round cultivation, board support and encouragement, a plan, an attainable goal, and lots of excitement.

That about says it.

13

The Philanthropic Journey

The charitable sector of our society is a rich tapestry of many diverse organizations serving unique and important social objectives. It is as vibrant as the underlying society it serves. It is a wonder to behold when you allow yourself some contemplative moments. Consider the wonder that DeTocqueville must have felt many, many years ago when he observed,

> I have come across several types of associations in America, of which, I confess, I had not previously the slightest conception, and I have often admired the extreme skills they show in proposing a common object for the exertions of very many and in inducing them voluntarily to pursue it.

Fund raisers are at the very core of that rather remarkable enterprise DeTocqueville observed.

The reason I like to spend so much time considering the dynamic of the philanthropic enterprise is precisely because it is so important. The same can be said of gaining an understanding of what motivates our volunteers and donors. I am a far better fund raiser because I have considered these issues and have utilized my findings and conclusions in my approach to relationship building.

It's easy to pontificate in a seminar or in a book as if I had operated with this knowledge for my many years of fund raising, but the truth is I had much of it wrong for so long. Still, I was able to raise money because I worked hard, maintained my integrity and represented an institution with a mission of importance. But I am certainly a better fund raiser because I have learned those things that I have attempted to share with you.

The dynamic of individual giving is even a marvel to behold at the micro level. I have seen the difference giving can make in the lives of others. I have observed firsthand the incredible joy and satisfaction which results from the positive giving experience. That is not to be taken lightly. There is truly something magical about it.

Jerry Panas' donors in *Mega Gifts* talked extensively about that magic. Once you give, you give again. Oddly enough, most of his donors also observed that their material success increased once they started giving. Don't say that too loud at a cocktail party, but I have noted the same thing. Somehow, when you open yourself up and give freely you receive even more in return. Payton Conway March summarized it when he said:

> There is a wonderful, mythical law of nature that the three things we crave most in life — happiness, freedom, and peace of mind — are always attained by giving them to someone else.

I suspect that the law March refers to is not really so mythical after all.

I am often asked by audiences why I am so enthusiastic about major gifts fund raising. I respond by saying that surely one aspect is the mental challenge. I love the permutations and possibilities involved in nurturing fund raising and in developing strategies for same. The possibilities are endless, and each situation is different. I even relish having to react to the uncertainties and surprises which inevitably arise with this type of endeavor. It's impossible to become bored because each situation and each move is unique. It must be so. Each one of our prospects is unique, and therefore, they react in a way which is particular to them. Add to it the nuances and complexities of giving methodology, and you have created a world of multiple challenges and opportunities.

Even more important than the mental challenge, however, is the human side of the equation. I think first of the colleagues with whom I am privileged to be associated. Development professionals are bright and by definition gregarious. They are just fun to be with. In addition, I think development professionals are sparked by a desire to accomplish something bigger than themselves. The effective fund raiser is driven and sustained by the important mission being served. Fund raisers could easily ply their talents and skills in another context, but outcomes are important to these professionals. That makes fund raisers very special "in my book" and I consider myself privileged to be among you.

The most important aspect of the human equation is our association with our donors. When you think of it, fund raising is really the process of asking people to share a dream or a vision. We ask our donors to consider the possibilities of a better world — to help us leave the world a bit better than when we came into it. We ask others to dream with us, to share our ideals and to help make what was once only thought possible become reality. We are privileged in our business to deal on a daily basis with people who care, who give freely of time and resources in order to achieve something worthwhile for generations yet to come. What a wonderful business it is when you recognize the privilege of such an association. Our donors are doing something special, and it is an honor to be associated with them.

In fund raising it is not the dollars raised, but the outcomes in human terms. Oh, we must measure ourselves in terms of dollars raised, but let's never forget the lives that are touched. Our donors are making a difference, and our satisfaction should come from being a part of that enterprise. What a thrill it is to be associated with these individuals.

Leo Rosten once said that, "The purpose of life is to matter, to count, to stand for something, to have it make some difference that we have lived at all." Our donors make a difference through their marvelous gifts. We as major gifts fund raisers can make a difference because of our association with them.

Let me tell you about my friend Bill. He and his rather remarkable wife, Evelyn, embarked on a philanthropic journey many years ago. Evelyn was a brilliant child psychologist, and Bill always marveled at her abilities. They set out on a course of supporting students at many different universities; Evelyn because of her educational leanings and Bill because of his admiration for her. Bill had always said that he wanted to nurture and encourage minds like Evelyn's. When Bill lost Evelyn he continued on his philanthropic path in her honor. Millions of dollars have been directed to important educational institutions because of their generosity. Thousands of worthy and deserving students will achieve an enhanced educational experience because Bill and Evelyn cared enough to seize opportunities.

I once remarked to Bill that he was one of the most successful people I had ever met. He demurred by observing that I was in constant contact with people of greater wealth and with more impressive titles. I told him that my definition of success was somewhat different from that. One evening in tribute to Bill and his philanthropic activities, I shared with him my definition of success. It came from Ralph Waldo Emerson.

> To laugh often and much;
> To win the respect of intelligent people
> and the affection of children;
> To earn the appreciation of honest critics
> and endure the betrayal of false friends;
> To appreciate beauty;
> To find the best in others;
> To leave the world a bit better whether by
> a healthy child, a garden patch, or a
> redeemed social condition;
> To know that even one life has breathed

easier because you have lived,
This is to have succeeded.

Our donors, through their gifts, succeed many times over when you use Emerson's litmus test. If we do our jobs well as development professionals, representing with integrity organizations of importance, it will be said of us that we have succeeded.

Indeed, it is important that we expend every effort to succeed as Emerson defined it because the philanthropic sector in a very real way is our hope for the future. It represents our aspirations and hopes. We should leave no stone unturned or effort unexpended in service of our important task. Victor Hugo said it best.

The future has several names.
For the weak it is impossible,
For the fainthearted it is unknown,
For the thoughtful and valiant it is ideal,
The challenge is urgent, the task is large.
The time is now.

I wish you well on your philanthropic journey.

Appendix

Fund Agreement

This AGREEMENT is made and entered into this _____ day of_____, 1992 between _____, of _____, _____ (hereinafter called the "Donor") and the _____, a not-for-profit corporation in the State of _____ (hereinafter called the "Corporation").

A. <u>Acknowledgment and Name of Gift.</u> The corporation, in acknowledgment of the fact that the Donor intends to make gifts from time to time to the Corporation, whether inter vivos or testamentary, for the purposes described herein, agrees to hold, administer, and distribute the property received as a result of said gifts as provided herein. The gifts shall be designated on the books and records of the Corporation as the "_____

_____ Fund" (hereinafter called the "Fund"). The Donor or any other person may at any time make additional contributions to the Fund by gift, Will, or otherwise.

B. <u>Investments</u>. The Corporation is authorized to continue investment of the Fund in the assets received as contributions to the Fund, or the Corporation may sell or exchange any of said assets and reinvest the proceeds in any manner it may deem fit.

C. <u>Income From Fund.</u> The principal of the Fund shall be held as an endowment and the net income therefrom shall be held and disposed of upon the terms and conditions prescribed herein.

    1.

    2.

    3.

D. <u>Alternate Application of Income.</u> In the event the <u>(your organization)</u> determines at some future time that it is no longer practical for the Fund to be used as specified herein, then the Corporation may devote the net income from the Fund to:

_____

_____

In any such alternate application of income, the funding source shall be clearly identified as the "_____

_____ Fund."

E. <u>Representatives and Successors Bound.</u> This Agreement shall be binding upon and inure to the benefit of the parties hereto, their heirs, executors, administrators, legal representatives, successors, and assigns.

IN WITNESS WHEREOF, the parties have causes this Agreement to be executed the day of the year hereinabove written.

(_____ NAME OF YOUR ORGANIZATION _____)

By: _____

_____

Its: _____ Executive Director _____

ATTEST:

APPROVED AS TO CONTENT:

Bibliography

Tony Alessandra, Ph.D, Phil Wesler and Rick Barrera; *Non- Manipulative Selling*; Simon and Schuster; 1984.

Tony Alessandra and Rick Barrera; *Collaborative Selling*; John Wiley & Sons, Inc.; 1993.

Robert R. Blake and Jane Srygley Mouton; *Guideposts For Effective Salesmanship*; Playboy Press; 1970.

Thomas E. Broce; *Fund Raising*; University of Oklahome Press; 1986.

Robert B. Cialdini; *Influence*; Quill: 1984.

Douglas M. Lawson; *Gift to Live*; ALTI; 1991.

Theodore Levitt; *The Marketing Imagination*; The Free Press; 1986.

Robert B. Miller and Stephen E. Herman; *Conceptual Selling*; Warner Books; 1987.

Jerold Panas; *Mega Gifts*; Bonus Books; 1984.

Jerold Panas; *Born to Raise*; Bonus Books; 1988.

Russ Alan Prince and Karen Maru File; *The Seven Faces of Philanthropy*; Josey-Bass; 1994.

Neil Rackham; *Major Account Sales Strategy*; McGraw-Hill; 1988.

Neil Rackham; *Spin Selling*; McGraw-Hill; 1988.

Peter M. Senge; *The Fifth Discipline*; Doubleday; 1990.

Gary Tobin; *American Jewish Philanthropy in the 90's*; Brandeis University Press; 1995.

Carl D. Zaiss and Thomas Gordon; *Sales Effectiveness Training*; Penguin Books; 1993.

Index

V

W

Z